Spiritual Reading For The
Biblical Christian

REVEREND ROBERT E. ALBRIGHT

SPIRITUAL READING FOR THE BIBLICAL CHRISTIAN
50 HOMILIES AND SERMONS

2008

Spiritual Reading For The Biblical Christian

CONTENTS

ACKNOWLEDGMENTS

I owe a great deal of gratitude to so many people whose influence, thoughts and even words can be found throughout my homilies and sermons.

First to all the living and deceased members of the teams of liturgists and preachers who have journeyed with me over the years: Dominicuskerk and Studenten Ekklessia in Amsterdam; Loyola College, St. Matthew Parish, Emmaus Community, and Towson University Newman Center in Baltimore.

To my friends and colleagues who have had a profound effect on my growth in preaching: Bernard Huijbers, Huub Oosterhuis, Father Felix Malmberg, SJ, Sister Cleophas Costello, RSM, Dr. Bernard Nachbahr, Dr. Pastor Norman Beck, Mary Marousek, and Father Joseph Bonadio, SS.

To the scholarly works and teachings of Father Raymond Brown, SS, Father Edward Schillebeeckx, OP, Father Xavier Leon-Dufour, SJ, Father Roger Balducelli, OSFS, Bishop John Shelby Spong, Rabbi Joseph Telushkin, Abraham Heschel, and many others too numerous to name here.

To Agnieszka Balawejder, my friend and computer consultant, and to all those who sat through these homilies and sermons and encouraged me to put them into print.

A debt of thanks to you all!

INTRODUCTION / PREFACE

I am now retired, having served in the Roman Catholic Church as a brother of the Christian Schools for thirteen years and as a priest for the past thirty-five years. My ministries included teaching high school and serving as a houseparent in an orphanage while with the brothers, working as an associate pastor in two parish churches, and serving as campus minister at three different colleges and universities since my ordination as a priest.

The following sermons and homilies are a sampling of my thirty-five years of preaching in the pulpit. I have adjusted many of these works to serve as spiritual reading for you, the reader. You will notice these writings are categorized as sermons and homilies—the difference being this: A **sermon** is a talk or essay that explores a particular religious topic or issue; a **homily** is a talk or essay that attempts to interpret a particular passage or passages of sacred Scripture in contemporary terms, applying it to the lives of the hearers or readers.

As you go through the pages ahead, you can spot a **homily** by the required reading passage(s) at the beginning of the essay. It will be necessary for the reader to have a Bible handy to read the cited passage(s) *before* embarking into the homily itself. The **sermons** have no particular Scripture required, but contain Scripture passages within the essay itself. Biblical quotations in this volume (unless otherwise noted) are taken from The New American Bible, 1988 translation.

Throughout the homilies and sermons, various noted spiritual writers will be quoted. Who they are and the sources of their words will be explained in the text itself, without the need for footnotes or the like. I hope this makes for easier reading without the distraction of going to the bottom of the page or to the rear of the book, causing the reader to lose track of the thoughts, which are most important.

My hope in producing this little volume is not only to preserve some of the work I have done, but also to share it again with previous hearers and to expand to an even wider audience. In each of these pieces, I have attempted to challenge, inspire, and give meaning to the life of each of you, the readers. I pray that will happen! Thank you for opening yourself to me and all those whose words are contained herein.

Sincerely,
Father Bob Albright
September 2008

1.
A BRIEF INTRODUCTION TO READING THE BIBLE

The Bible is not a history book, though it contains historical material. It is not a science book, though it contains the scientific knowledge of that time. It is not a philosophy book, though many philosophies are put forth. It is not a theology book, since there are many conflicting theologies in it. It is not a journal of events, though it may seem that way at times. It is not an answer book; Father Raymond Brown, the renowned Roman Catholic American scripture scholar, once said: "Asking the question, what does the Bible say about a certain topic, is like asking, what does the Library of Congress say about it."

If the Bible is "not" all of these things, then what is it? **The Bible is a book of faith.** It is the faith of Israel, of the Jews, of Christians, of the Church. It is revelation. It is the word of God. When reading or studying or discussing the Bible, one must always keep this fundamental point in mind. And so, I repeat it: **The Bible is a book of faith!**

The Bible contains literature of many different genres to express its faith: Stories, parables, letters, dramas, liturgies, memoirs, legal codes, songs, prose, poetry, epics, sagas, prophecies, myths, proverbs, and much more. Consequently, reading the Bible becomes a process of association of images and symbols, such as light and darkness, gardens and deserts, water and thirst, bread and wine, and many more. It is one story made up of many different stories, written in many different places, at many different times, by many different people.

Therefore, the Bible cannot always be taken literally—but it can still be taken as truth! The stories of the Bible cannot always be taken as historical, literal events like a news account of today or a media description of the news. The word of God, as well as the words of humans, is contained in the Bible. Not every verse can be the word of God.

All of this is so foreign to the modern American mind-set. We are a literal and technological society. The storytelling culture that produced the Bible is often far from our experience as modern-day dwellers, and that means we need a new pair of glasses with which to read this unique book.

Modern biblical scholarship is rather new. After almost two thousand years of reading the Bible literally, we are being asked to look at these documents through the eyes of those who wrote them. Through archaeology, historical and literary critique, we know more today about the first century of the Common Era than the people who lived in it. We need to apply what we are learning to our modern-day reading of the Bible. That's what I will be doing in the pages ahead. You must know this before you embark on the journey this book sets forth. Also, I will be using the scholarly way of referring to biblical ages: CE refers to the Common Era, from Jesus to the present day; BCE refers to before the Common Era, before the time of Jesus. The "Biblical Christian" is one who will be open to this scholarship and be able to grow in faith even in the face of this book's challenges.

Faith, I believe, is going beyond the facts! Therefore, if the Bible is a book of faith, the reader will have to go beyond the facts of science and history to a very different level. The reader will have to learn to go beyond the sometime nonliteral, nonscientific, nonhistorical approach of these ancient authors and effect the leap of faith they are calling every reader to make. The author of the fourth Gospel in the New Testament sums it all up, when at the end of his Gospel he declares: "Now Jesus did many other signs in the presence of his disciples that are not written in this book. But these are written that you may **come to believe** that Jesus is the Messiah, the Son of God, and that through **this belief** you may have life in his name" (John 20:30-31).

2.
MODERN BIBLICAL SCHOLARSHIP

Readings: Sirach 3:17-24 Luke 14:1, 7-14

When anyone approaches a Scripture passage to interpret it, there are two basic things that must happen: **Exegesis** and **hermeneutics**. Those two big "scripture scholar" words simply mean the following:

Exegesis—what is actually going on in the passage at the time it was written. **Hermeneutics**—what this passage says to me today.

Exegesis—means "uncover."

Hermeneutics—means "apply."

So first, we **uncover** what the original meaning and intention of the passage was. Second, we **apply** the passage to our own lives.

Let me give you an example from the Gospel of Luke above how to do this. The famous Belgian systematic theologian, Father Edward Schillebeeckx, notes that in most of Jesus' teachings there is the mention of food or meals. Also, that the characters in most parables seem to be wealthy people with servants, etc. This is exegesis. Schillebeeckx concludes or "uncovers" the circumstance in which this parable or teaching occurs—Jesus was at a meal in the house of a wealthy person. Jesus does nothing but simply look around himself and finds plenty of material on which to teach or speak a parable. Evidently, that is why he had been invited in the first place. The rich found a curiosity in Jesus, this itinerant teacher, and in their curiosity invited him into their homes to experience his teaching and what sort of person he was.

The next level of exegesis is to remember whose Gospel we are reading—in this case, the Gospel according to Luke. No other Gospel contains this story and teaching in exactly this way. The only similarity in other Gospels is the phrase "whoever is exalted will be humbled and whoever is humbled will be exalted."

While on the surface, this looks like a simple lesson in humility—it is anything but that in the way Luke constructs the story. This story in Luke is a polemic—that is, a construction to show tension between two poles. The obvious polemic is between Jews and Gentiles. The Jews (clear, in that it was a Pharisee's house) are claiming to be the inheritors of God's kingdom and demanding the higher places in that kingdom (which is always described or symbolized by a banquet in the Hebrew Scriptures). The Christians (the Gentiles in Luke's community) are being denied any place of honor in that kingdom (or banquet). When the Scripture uses the term "Gentiles," it means non-Jews, all nations outside of Israel.

The polemic in Luke is clear when the host is told not to invite friends and neighbors to his banquet, but rather the outcasts. This is not a polemic between good Jews and bad Jews. It is a polemic between the insiders and the outsiders. Gentiles were outsiders—even in Christianity, which eventually became totally Gentile. Luke's Gospel is a Gospel for the outcasts, the rejected, "the Anawim," written in Southern Greece approximately 80 CE.

Now, how do we apply this Gospel to our lives? We begin our hermeneutics, or application, by discarding Luke's application of this teaching and go directly to the teaching of Jesus. The Jew/Gentile polemic was not known to Jesus. Jesus spoke only to Jews! Jesus was a Jew! He was never concerned with polemics between Jews and Gentiles. Luke, however, was.

Having "uncovered" this, we can "apply" the passage more accurately to ourselves by using Jesus' lesson in humility given to his brother and sister Jews. Instead of a polemic between two groups, we can discover the selfishness of individual people—no matter what race or religion they may be. Jesus, a Jew, admonishes his own brother and sister Jews. Luke, a Gentile, throws stones at the Jews. Jesus utilizes humility in self-critique. Luke criticizes others.

The hermeneutics are clear. How we must apply this to our lives: be humble enough to recognize our own limitations before criticizing the limitations of others; be humble enough to take less and give more; be humble enough to do for others even if they do nothing for you in return; be humble enough to give the other person the benefit of the doubt; be humble enough to know the questions and not the answers; be humble enough not to jump to conclusions.

The virtue of humility is essential to being a Christian. Because being a Christian is being open and humble enough to accept change and new things. As Christians, we are humbled in the face of knowledge and the pursuit of truth!

And so I close by reminding you of the advice given by the author of the reading from the Book of Sirach: "Conduct your affairs with humility and you will be loved more than the giver of gifts. Humble yourself, the more, the greater you are, and you will find favor with God."

3.
INSPIRATION IN THE BOOK OF GENESIS

Readings: Genesis 3:1-24 Ephesians 1:3-6 Luke 1:26-38

Every once in a while, someone will ask: "Isn't the Bible supposed to be inspired by God? What does inspiration mean? How did God inspire the Bible?"

I teach three or four different Bible classes every year and yet I never attempt to answer these questions directly. I never define inspiration for them, and so I won't for you either.

The concept of inspiration is not something that is "taught," but "caught."

There are hundreds of places in the Bible where one can "catch" this concept; and one of them is in the reading listed above—the story of the fall of Adam and Eve.

One cannot define "inspiration," but we can at least point to it now and then, hoping that somehow you will "catch" the meaning of it, as preserved by the Church since the beginning.

Let's look at the reading from Genesis: Adam and Eve eat from the forbidden tree—they immediately hide—God finds them and questions them—Adam blames Eve, Eve blames the serpent—all three are eventually punished.

That's the story!—What is it saying?

What it says is much more complicated and involved than the surface details of a story, because it is not just a story, but *the* story of every man and woman who has ever lived on this earth.

This story is a psychological drama of the internal struggle that is experienced by all people who taste the reality of living. It is the story of the emerging conscience that every child discovers at some point in life—the point where we are no longer comfortable running around the house or the backyard naked, but "grow up" to the awareness of being nude. It is the story of the conscience speaking to the human person, helping to discover right from wrong, walking proudly when we think we're right and hiding when we think we're wrong. It is the story of guilt—that feeling we get when we disobey or do something wrong. It is the story of blame—passing the buck—as comedian Flip Wilson used to say, "The devil made me do it." It is the story of punishment—of learning how to live with the consequences of our actions. It is the story of the human person's freedom to choose, even wrongly. It is the story of good and evil—the struggle that goes on inside and outside each one of us with every choice we make. It is the story of sin!

The science of psychology has only flourished in the past hundred years or so—it is still an infant science—so much about the human person is still unknown. Yet, more than two thousand years ago the story of Adam and Eve was written in a culture where psychology as a science was virtually unheard of; but it *was* written, not accidentally, but skillfully, describing the most complicated components of the human person: conscience, will, guilt, blame, intellect, emotions, the mind, the human psyche!

If it were possible for you to meet the author of that story and commend him on his use of psychology, he would have no idea what you were talking about.

And that's where we get a glimpse of what it means to say that the Bible is inspired!

Yet, God's inspiration is not that easily detectable. No one can say what it means when God "inspires" the Bible, just as no one can say who God is! To say, then, that you were inspired to do this or that by God is not yours to say—it takes more than that—it takes a community—and even more, a community of faith to determine inspiration. The first community to do this in our history was Israel. The second community to do this was the early Christians. The community who still does this today is us Christians in union with all Christians and Muslims and Jews around the world.

The same inspiration found in the Old Testament is found in the New Testament. The same inspiration found in the Bible is found in the Christian Church. The same inspiration that produced the untimely story of a man and woman who have the ability to sin in the Book of Genesis produces another untimely story in the Christian Scripture—the story of a man and a woman conceived without sin.

The same inspiration that exposes the human condition expresses the human vision: In the New testament, Jesus becomes the New Adam. Mary becomes the New Eve.

In other words, sin will not have the last word. The human person was created with the ability to sin, but not the destiny to sin. Our abilities are symbolized in the persons of Adam and Eve. Our destiny is symbolized in the persons of Jesus and Mary—who were conceived like the man and woman in the first story of creation, "In the image and likeness of God" (Gen. 1:27).

Do you find this all a little far-fetched for us or even Mary? Then listen to these other words of inspiration once again: "God chose us (**us**) in Jesus before the foundation of the world, to be holy and without blemish before him" (Eph.)..."for nothing will be impossible for God" (Luke).

4.
THE BABYLONIAN CAPTIVITY: WHAT WAS IT?

Readings: Jeremiah 52:1-30 Lamentations 1:1-22 Psalm 80

The Lord has become an enemy, he has consumed Israel...the roads to Sion mourn...the Lord has punished her for her many sins...gone from daughter Sion is all her glory...how lonely she is now, the once crowded city...Jerusalem is defiled...come, all you who pass by the way, look and see whether there is any suffering like my suffering. Shepherd of Israel, hear our prayer...rescue us...how long yet will you turn angrily away? Look down on this vine...why were its fences destroyed? Be here among us..."

What a blow it must have been for Judah to have Jerusalem and the temple destroyed! What a tragedy it must have been for it to have produced so many woes, psalms, and lamentations! What a crisis it must have been to have stirred even shepherds to become prophets!

From all that is written in the Old Testament, one gets the impression that no other event in the history of the world could have been as degrading as this one. The lifestyle of this people changed; the geography of this people changed; the honor of this people changed; even the name of this people changed. When the Babylonian army destroyed Israelite independence and marched the people into exile in 587 BCE, they struck at the very heart of biblical life. The Babylonians demolished what seemed essential to the religion of Israel and therefore thought to be indestructible—the temple and its ritual, the city of Jerusalem, the possession of the Promised Land, and the privileges of the Davidic royalty. The "Israelite" was to be henceforth called the "Jew."

For the moment, let us dwell on what actually happened. Remembering, of course, that at this time in the history of Israel, there were two kingdoms (the Northern Kingdom called "Israel" and the Southern Kingdom called "Judah"), and the events occurred as follows: In the Northern Kingdom of "Israel," their fall came rapidly following the death of King Jeroboam II in 746 BCE. His son and heir to the throne was murdered within six months and anarchy began to reign in this Northern Kingdom. Anyone was king and no one knew who was boss. This made the kingdom extremely vulnerable, and the Assyrians (the greatest power at this point in history) took the advantage. Bit by bit, the Northern Kingdom fell into the hands of the Assyrians until its chief city (Samaria) was besieged in 721 BCE and all of the Northern Kingdom became a province of the Assyrian empire with an Assyrian governor. Some of the Israelites were deported to Assyria and many Assyrians settled in Israel.

Slowly, the Assyrians moved into the Southern Kingdom of "Judah." Around 612 BCE, the empire of Babylonia ascended to world power, conquering both Assyria and Egypt. "Judah" became caught in the power play among these large nations due to the ineffectual and irreligious reign of King Jehoiakim (609-598 BCE). Nebuchadnezzar, king of the Babylonians, eventually besieged Jerusalem in 589 BCE and devastated the rest of the Southern Kingdom. In 587 BCE, the walls of Jerusalem were breached, the temple destroyed, and large deportations ensued. The people from the Southern Kingdom of "Judah" were exiled to Babylon and Egypt.

This is what we call: the Babylonian captivity or the Babylonian exile. This exile or captivity lasted about forty-eight years (587-539 BCE).

Exiled in Babylon and Egypt, with nothing left but the word of the Torah (the Law) and the threats of the persecuted prophets, the people of Israel meditated long and hard upon that word and those threats. This meditation was genuine, realistic, and heroic, and it expressed itself in the writings of the Prophet Ezekiel and the unknown poet-prophet we call Second Isaiah.

While in exile, the old thought patterns of Israel dissolved and were reshaped in new ways. This period witnessed intense religious activity on the part of these newly called "Jews." Israel's traditions were gathered and committed to writing. The Torah was given form by a new school of writers (called the Priestly writers today). The historical books of the Old Testament were edited and the writings of the prophets were collected. The Prophet Ezekiel spoke of Israel's resurrection (Ezek. 37:1-14), but it was the "unknown" prophet and his followers who supplied the spark for Israel to return. Second Isaiah, as he is called today, knew that Israel's punishment was at an end, and King Cyrus of Persia was the "anointed one" or messiah of the Lord who would secure Israel's return (Isa. 44:24-28; 45:1-7).

By 539 BCE, Second Isaiah's prophecies came to pass as the Persians (under the leadership of Cyrus) conquered the Babylonians. Cyrus was a man of great religious tolerance, and in 538 BCE he issued a decree allowing the exiles to return to the land of Israel.

Thus ended the exile! There followed a great period of rebuilding in Israel with the restoration of the temple in 515 BCE. But more important, was the rebuilding of Israel's faith, hopes, and dreams. This came in the widespread attempt to put into writing much of their oral tradition. Most of the Old Testament, as we know it today, was either written or edited in this restoration period. Therefore, much of the Old Testament writing is colored by the exile crisis. Much of the Old Testament reflects the feelings of a people who were in exile, yet returned home still dreaming, singing, and carrying sheaves on their shoulders, as if they had only gone out to do a day's work in the fields!

The exile (apparent from the Old Testament writings) had a profound effect on the life of Israel. They began to see things more clearly. They began to understand the past and the covenant with new eyes. There was a new surge of courage. The future began to take shape. A new life awaited them. And it seemed that the prophecy of Ezekiel had come true, for Israel had risen from the dead. Though it was one of the most critical and divisive tragedies in Israel's history, the exile became the most central and decisive. It seemed to produce fruit. One is led to believe from all this, that to tear down and rebuild occasionally is a good thing! In the darkness of the exile, the "Light" of the Hebrew Scriptures came into being!

5.
PROPHECY AND APOCALYPTICISM DURING THE EXILE

Reading: Ezekiel 1:1-28; 2:1-10; 3:1-27

There are three major developments that took place for Israel during the exile that I would like to deal with: Firstly, the problem of the presence of God; secondly, the effect that the Babylonian people, culture, and beliefs had on Israel; and thirdly, the change from prophetic writing to apocalyptic literature.

Realizing that the Temple was destroyed and that it stood for centuries in their midst as a tangible sign of God's presence and favor, the obvious question arose among the exiles: Where is God now? The answer to this question developed slowly and, as usual, it came from the prophets and their prophecy. Jeremiah, who was left behind in Judah for a while during the exile and later deported to Egypt, wrote these words to the exiles in Babylon: "Thus says the Lord...when you call me, when you go to pray to me, I will listen to you. When you look for me, you will find me...you will find me with you" (Jer. 29:12-13). Second Isaiah, the unknown poet-prophet of the exile wrote: "Comfort, give comfort to my people says your God...Go up onto a high mountain...and cry out...here is your God!...Like a shepherd he feeds his flock" (Isaiah 40:1,9,11).

The answer the prophets gave to this question was that God was in Babylon. God is where his people are. God is with his people. Not in the temple of fancy, or in the mausoleums built in his honor, but God is right here in our midst, here in the shadow of hope. Their theology began to revert back to the Covenant theology whereby they believed that God is no longer just their God, but that they were God's people. They were becoming people of God again, because they were becoming believers and not just builders and ritualizers. God is the One who is with the remnant that keep the faith. Happy the person who believes. Happy the tree near the spring. This God is a God who finds a home in **all** people who believe, not just in Judah, but even on the alien soil of Babylon. God is a stranger without any race.

It was not only the words of the prophets that became a sign that God was present among the exiles, but also the very existence of prophets outside of Israel. Letters from Jeremiah and the prophet we call Second Isaiah (in exile himself) were signs of God's care for his people in exile. But the most important sign came in the Prophet Ezekiel. Among the first to be deported from Judah before the destruction of Jerusalem and the temple were the priests. One of these priests was a man named Ezekiel. Shortly after deportation, Ezekiel, now in Babylon, married a woman from Judah and lived as Jeremiah had exhorted—building a home, planting a farm, herding sheep, etc. (Jer. 29:5-6). As described in the reading above, Ezekiel was called by God to be a prophet in Babylon by the river Chebar. Ezekiel is the only prophet of Israel who was called to prophecy outside the Promised Land. The very act of God calling a man to prophecy in a foreign land was a sign to the exiles that God had not forgotten them. Shortly after the call of Ezekiel to prophecy, the city of Jerusalem fell and the temple was destroyed; countless more Jews were deported to Babylon.

While in exile, Ezekiel became a rallying force behind much of the development of new thought among the exiles. He gathered them in prayer on the Sabbath and at other times, thus beginning the new concept of *synagogue*. The idea of praying outside the temple was a new one and one that would become a permanent lifestyle for the Jews from when they returned from exile until the present day. Ezekiel encouraged study, writing, praying, and research among the exiles. He, himself, began a new literary trend called the Priestly writers, which would effect a change in biblical writing and add a whole new dimension to Jewish theology.

These changes and new dimensions included taking many myths and tales of the Babylonians and turning them into biblical narratives, with Jewish theology and a Jewish philosophy that drastically altered the original myth. An example of this would be the first creation story that is found in the Book of Genesis, chapter one. This narrative or hymn was taken from the ancient Babylonian tale called "Enuma elish." The biblical narrative of Noah and the ark stems from the Babylonian myth called "Gilgamesh." The Priestly writers took these tales and formed them with the theology of Israel—one God—instead of the many gods, which was the theology of Babylon.

One of the greatest literary developments at this time came in the writings of Ezekiel himself. His book of prophecies is mixed with prophetic writing and apocalyptic writing. With the Book of Ezekiel comes the style of literature we call "apocalyptic." Apocalyptic means literally "that which will soon happen."

Because apocalyptic writing grew out of prophecy, and because this development occurred during the exile, and because the Book of Ezekiel is a good example of this development, then it is most appropriate for us to speak about apocalyptic writing in this sermon. Let us begin with some comparisons and contrasts: The prophets were men of action—apocalyptists were men of the written word; the prophets were personally involved in the politics of their day—the apocalyptists looked to a more cosmic mission; the prophets presented their message as a judgment upon individual events—the apocalyptists developed a religious explanation of universal history; the prophets were concerned with Israel—the apocalyptists were concerned with a worldwide vision; the prophets spoke bluntly about religious abuses and were seldom misunderstood—the apocalyptists wrote symbolically about "visions" that they themselves did not fully understand and that their audiences and readers found even more baffling.

Symbolism, in fact, is one of the most characteristic traits of apocalyptic writing. Almost everything of this earth was used symbolically. The parts of the human body had their value: eyes symbolized knowledge; hands, power; legs, stability; white hair, antiquity or majesty; mouth, divine oracle. Animals counted also for symbolism: The lion for royalty; the ox for strength; the eagle for swiftness; the dragon or sea monster for evil; the lamb for sacrifice; the horns of an animal for power; the wings of a bird for agility. Clothing too was symbolic. Colors possessed a symbolic status very similar to liturgical colors in many Christian traditions: white for joy or victory; red for martyrdom; scarlet for luxury. Finally, even numbers received symbolism: Four symbolized the corners of the created world; seven or forty symbolized perfection; twelve symbolized the new Israel or people of God; one thousand symbolized multitude.

Prophetic writing insisted on a "Day of the Lord" with sweeping darkness upon the wicked and bringing victory to the elect. Apocalyptic literature saw the darkness still deeper and the light still more blinding;

goodness and evil were interlocked in mortal struggle. Prophetic writing saw the present as a sorrowful moment leading to a future victory. Apocalyptic literature watched the heavens open and the future crash into the present.

The two key figures in the onward evolution of prophecy into apocalyptic literature are Ezekiel and the author of Daniel. Ezekiel managed to divert this movement away from the moralizing role of the prophets toward an emphasis on liturgical renewal. Being a priest, he combined his liturgical expertise with his prophetic vocation and transformed both into apocalyptic literature. Later, the author of the Book of Daniel liberated apocalyptic literature from the grasp of priestly writers and standardized it as a literature for laity and clergy alike.

Apocalypticism, then, can be briefly characterized as an exilic and postexilic development of prophetic style, in which heavenly secrets about the universe and the end of time are revealed in symbolic form. These symbols are explained by angels to a visionary who writes down his message under the pseudonym of some ancient personage. Thus, you can see now how the reading above from Ezekiel is apocalyptic.

There were, then, as I explained earlier, three major developments that took place for Israel during the exile. The exile taught Israel that God was with them no matter where they lived, as long as they believed and remembered the covenant. The exile gave the Israelites new knowledge and materials in theology and philosophy upon which they could form their own scriptures. Finally, the exile produced Ezekiel, the "Father of Judaism" (as he is called today), and his writings produced a whole new development from prophecy to apocalyptic literature.

All this turned the "Israelites" into "Jews." All this turned the "Jews" into the "people of God." And, after all, that's what they were in the beginning, are now, and ever shall be, world without end. Amen!

6.
PSALM 72

Reading: Psalm 72:1-17

Let me begin by posing a question to you about this psalm: Who is the "he" in this psalm? The original psalm calls him a king:
"Give your wisdom, God, to the king,
lay your kingdom in his hands,
that he may be a shepherd for your people,
for your poor people a righteous judge." (From *Fifty Psalms* by Huub Oosterhuis)

But I still ask: who is the "he" in Psalm 72?...Other books in the Old Testament, such as the prophets, call him messiah.

For centuries, Christians have always had Jesus in mind when they recited this psalm.

The poet, the psalmist, just calls him "he."

And so once more I ask you: Who is the "he" in this psalm? Some great hero? God? The president of the United States? The pope?

Notice what is said about this "he": He will live and never fail! He brings peace in abundance! His name lasts for ever! His name goes around the earth from person to person! He is within reach! Who answers to these praises? No one! No one person! No one is God! Not even God is one person!

Why is it that we people are always looking for someone who is it! Someone who will do it for us! Someone who will save us! We are always looking for someone, a king, a saint, a pope, a president, a prophet. That nostalgia is always at work in us—a patient with her doctor, a pupil with his teacher, a daughter with her mother, a wife with her husband, a friend with a friend, a penitent with his confessor. It never ends. We go on and on looking for heroes, that someone who holds the key to life, who has all the answers, who is a superman, a bionic woman, mighty mouse, wonder-worker, a guru. Probably some of you are reading this book with this same nostalgia, this same expectation.

We do it so much that we are not even conscious of it. And as we engage in this nostalgia, we put pressure on those someones. Poor someone, anyone, who is weighted down beneath the longings and illusions of others. Poor strong man. All blind hostilities, every disappointment will make you their target. Poor superstar. You will be blamed for the bondage and the failures of others. Or you will be forced to become corrupt to save yourself. Poor mighty-of-the-earth, choking on your own power—the power given so easily by nostalgic people who always want someone to do it for them, to be what they *think* they cannot be.

Since the beginning of time, we people, have been engaged in seeking out the someones of our world who will take upon themselves the tasks that we are not willing to do ourselves. In Psalm 72 this same nostalgia is at work: *He* will stand up for the poor and the needy. *He* will break and bind the powers which are holding us (not "I" but "He"). *He* gives hope to those without rights. *He* ransoms them from the house of slavery (not "I" but "He").

No generation is more engaged in this fantasy as we are today— paying taxes, dropping money in the basket, giving the kids a few bucks—then our problems are solved—we sit back and do nothing.

Even though Psalm 72 was written over two thousand years ago, it still has a prophetic voice in our midst today. The psalms are above time and circumstance. They speak of a "time" that has not yet arrived, and they speak of "circumstances" that are not yet fulfilled. Certainly when Psalm 72 was written, it was concerned specifically with a new king for Jerusalem. Yet in this psalm echoes the voice of Israel's conscience. And in that conscience is rooted the vision of a different world order, a vision which says: "Everybody or nobody"!

Slowly we begin to receive glimpses of the answer to my initial question. Centuries have given answers through heroes, gods, and spiritual leaders. Yet the psalm is still sung today. A hope and dream are still unfulfilled, and leaders and kings and queens and saints and presidents and prophets and gods and messiahs have come and gone. These someones do not seem to be the answers we need. These someones do not take death off our shoulders. These someones are not the "he" in Psalm 72!

The **he** in this psalm is **us**—you and me together. If this psalm has anything to say to us today, it is this: Everybody or nobody, all or nothing, one alone cannot save himself or herself. "He" is people, a body with hands and feet and a head. In other words, he is everyone or he is no one. It is not the person in power who is the focus, the beginning and the end, but the psalmist says: Dare to look at the humble, the poor, widows, those without rights, orphans, your neighbor, all people.

In our book, our Bible, that "he" is described over and over again. He is a child, a servant, powerless, alpha and omega. He is without figure or splendor, formless with no beauty in him. But upon him rests the spirit of God. In him dwells fullness. He is God-of-the-poor. He is the deprived for whom he stands up. He becomes the least among people. He is within reach, the person who is next to you, a person with whom to live, a word of peace, dryer of tears, a person of flesh, fragile as a flower, one who gives, taking us as his bride, unmasking all pride, giving in great abundance to the hungry.

Who is the he in Psalm 72? He is you. He is me. He is us. He is people. He is a body that lives for others. He is the Body of Christ!

And so my brothers and sisters, my friends and fellow believers, you know the conclusion to which we have come about this psalm. Just so there will be no mistake about it, permit me to express it for us: There will be no peace; faithfulness and truth will not flourish; the mountains will not yield sheaves of peace; the hills will not bear a harvest of justice—until you and I and every man, woman, and child who lives is within reach—until you and I and every man, woman, and child who lives stands up for the poor and the needy—until all people break and bind the powers that are holding us. Then we will be like the sun (son)! We will never fail! We **will** live!

7.
THE CONCEPT OF WISDOM IN THE BIBLE

There are seven books of the Old Testament that are classified as "Wisdom Books." In Hebrew they are called "The Writings" (*Khetuvim*). The word for "wisdom" in Hebrew is *hokmah*, and in Greek it is *sophia*. The reason for using both languages is that some of these books were written in Hebrew and some in Greek. The Greek books were never accepted into the Hebrew Bible (*Tanach*), simply because they were not written in the language the Jews considered sacred (i.e., Hebrew). When Martin Luther translated the Bible into the German language (1521-1534), he used the Hebrew version of the Old Testament (*Tanach*), which did not contain those Wisdom Books written originally in Greek. That is why in many protestant versions of the Bible these Greek books are missing, and yet they can be found in Catholic and Orthodox versions of the Bible since they use the Greek version of the Old Testament known as the *Septuagint*.

The seven books of wisdom in the Old Testament are: **Job,** written in Hebrew somewhere between the seventh and fifth centuries BCE; **Psalms,** written in Hebrew mostly before the third century BCE; **Proverbs,** written in Hebrew around the fifth century BCE; **Ecclesiastes,** written in Hebrew sometime in the third century BCE; **Song of Songs,** written in Hebrew around 538 BCE; **Wisdom,** written in Greek somewhere in the first century BCE; **Sirach,** written in Greek between 200-175 BCE.

The origin of "wisdom sayings" came from instructions or teachings about life and conduct transmitted from teacher to student or from parent to child or from monarch to heir. The purpose was to train a worthy ruler or courtly education and comes from ancient Egyptian, Babylonian, and Eastern Oriental thought. The wisdom literature, unlike all the other writings in the Bible is international.

The use by Israel and incorporation of these types of sayings into the Bible came mainly *after* the Babylonian exile (500-100 BCE). At that juncture in the history of Israel, you remember, there was no monarchy or royal court. The temple and Jerusalem were destroyed. The exiles were returning slowly back to their land and rebuilding their lives. Israel attached a religious quality to these teachings and moved this type of education into the family setting. Some connections were kept to the royal nature of these sayings because the time of King Solomon was looked upon as the "golden age of Israel's past" (965-926 BCE) and his memory was connected to the "building of the temple" and the fact that he was known as "a wise king," so the writers attached his name to many of the wisdom books. Naming a book after a famous person was a way of securing attention to the book and its message, even though the famous person did not live at the time the book was written.

Wisdom is a very elusive concept and we find scholars today using it in various ways. **Wisdom is the ability to integrate oneself into the existing order of things in a harmonious manner.** The opposite is "folly" and chaos, which is intolerable. This is not a shallow idea. It raises more questions than it answers. What if the existing order of things is a mess or unjust or downright evil?

A typical example of wisdom versus folly in our own world could be the experience of being stuck in a traffic jam. The wise person recognizes that there is nothing one can do to change the situation. The wise person integrates him or herself into the existing order of things in a harmonious manner. He or she remains calm and takes advantage of the slow-moving pace to renew oneself both inwardly and outwardly. The foolish person gets worked up into a frenzy and starts shifting from lane to lane (going nowhere) and might even yell a few nasty remarks out the window at undeserving bystanders. The foolish person has not integrated him or herself into the existing order of things and everything becomes far from harmonious.

Wisdom is a divine attribute of God freely given to our human nature. We, however, have the freedom to choose it or be foolish. Which will it be? When you get the chance, read some of the Wisdom Books in the Hebrew Scripture and learn more about how to be a wise person.

8.
THE FORMATION OF THE NEW TESTAMENT

If we look at New Testament times, and specifically the letters and gospels of our Scripture, we discover writings that cover three generations of Christians—the first three generations of Christians known to us. Let me examine briefly those three generations to show you how the New Testament was formed.

The first generation of Christians would begin with Jesus and go to about the year 70 CE (30-70 CE). The first generation of Christians would be the eyewitnesses to the events in the life of Jesus of Nazareth. The first generation of Christians would be those who knew Jesus personally and would include the twelve apostles, St. Paul, the seventy-two disciples, the ministering women, the first church at Jerusalem. The emerging leader in this first generation was the **apostle**—one who was sent to preach and speak the Gospel, the Good News. All questions and conflicts regarding the life of the Church in this first generation were referred to the apostles. All churches established in this first generation were done so by apostles (either one of the twelve or lesser known apostles). We could conclude, then, that the center of origin, unity, and leadership in the first-generation church was the apostle. And the apostle was one who **spoke** the Good News.

After approximately 70 CE, we move into second-generation Christianity (70-100 CE). All the apostles were dead. The eyewitnesses were no longer around. Those who could speak about their personal relationship with Jesus were gone. Only their children or relatives or friends or baptized brothers and sisters remained. Within this second generation of Christians, a new need arose. Since no one could speak the Gospel personally, the need to write down the spoken word emerges. Thus, Evangelists arose among various Christian communities around the Mediterranean region. These Evangelists replaced the apostles with their leadership through their authoritative writing down of the events in the life of Jesus. **Evangelists** acquired their authority by **writing** down the spoken words of the apostles, who were the eyewitnesses. Therefore, from approximately 70-100 CE, Evangelists were the successors of the Apostles in second-generation Christianity. We know them well. We don't really know who they were exactly, but we use the names which third-generation Christians gave them: Mark, Matthew, Luke, and John.

The third generation of Christianity begins approximately 90 CE and goes into the second century. We now have both apostles and Evangelists gone. The eyewitnesses who **spoke** the Good News and their successors who **wrote** the Good News are dead. Therefore, a new need arises to perpetuate, preserve, and teach the written word, to canonize and establish a Scripture, a Bible that became the word of God. The center of authority in this third generation was placed on those who would remain faithful to this Scripture, read it publicly and teach it with the fullness of personal faith. Two very such persons rise to prominence in two different parts of the world: Clement in Rome, approximately 96 CE, and Ignatius in Antioch, approximately 100 CE. Third generations of Christians placed leadership in men who were called episcopoi or boss or **Bishop.** These episcopoi were the ones who were responsible to be the chief **teachers** of the Good News, the source of unity around which the Christian community lived, grew, and survived. Therefore, in third-generation Christianity, the Bishops emerge as successors of the Evangelists, who were the successors of the Apostles.

In summary, then, the **apostle** of the first generation **spoke** the Good News; the **Evangelist** of the second generation **wrote** down the spoken word; the **Bishop** of the third generation **taught** the written word—all three always preserving the Good News for future generations.

This analysis, even though simple and brief, outlines how the New Testament came into being along with the structure in the early church. Therefore, it becomes clear to say that the writers of the New Testament were not eyewitnesses of the Jesus event. Only one eyewitness makes his appearance in the New Testament—and that is Paul. The four gospels and many of the letters received their names by the second-century church, who would be third-generation Christianity. This would be done by a council of the leaders of the local churches throughout the Christian world, who came to be known as bishops.

The role of bishop has changed dramatically over the past eighteen hundred years. When the Church took on imperial status in the fourth century, so too did the bishops. From the role of authority through teaching, the bishop became a ruler, similar to a governor. The pope (the bishop of Rome) became a ruler, similar to a king. The centrality of the Church in Rome comes from the New Testament because of its strong faith attested to by Paul in his Letter to the Romans (Rom. 1:8). All the trappings that went with the monarchy gradually found their way into the episcopacy—genuflection, kissing of hands, bows, rings, coats of arms, miters and crosiers, regal vestments, and titles. As Christianity became the religion of Europe, the bishop's role as monarch grew. By the Middle Ages, bishops were land owners and lords of castles. Slowly, the role of bishop moved from teacher to ruler and eventually to administrator.

Despite the quirks of history, the essential role of the bishop has always remained a leadership role, a sign of unity in the local church. The local church is the origin of the universal Church and the bishop is the center of the local church. Christianity has always been this kind of church—one that is formed from the bottom up and not from the top down.

9.
THE BIRTH STORIES OF JESUS

Readings: Matthew 1:1-2:23 Luke 1:5-2:40

The stories about the birth of Jesus are probably the first stories that were ever told to us as children! We know them in detail, even in details that do not exist in the stories themselves, but have been added by fantasy—such as the ox and donkey, the snow and wintry cold, the three kings, the crippled shepherd boy, and the stable. Perhaps we have added so much fantasy that we can hardly recognize these stories in their original form. Perhaps we have added so much that we no longer can discover any meaning in these stories. Therefore, let me help you put meaning back into them.

To begin with, each of the four Gospels was written in the reverse order one finds in the Bible today. It is evident from the preaching of Paul and the other apostles that the good news is Jesus, who suffered, died, was buried, and rose from the dead. This was the focal point of all preaching in apostolic times and therefore became the first stories formulated and recorded about Jesus. The passion, death, and resurrection sequences of the gospels came first. The stories of Jesus' ministry, words, and miracles all came later as amplification of the Easter story and also as a result of the resurrection theology. Finally each gospel writer or writers saw the need to introduce his audience and readers to the person of Jesus in a way that would sum up the whole gospel story, the Good News. The first gospel writer, Mark, doesn't seem to find this approach necessary and therefore begins his gospel immediately with Jesus' ministry. The writer of the fourth and last gospel, John, begins with a prologue, a liturgical hymn, and thus introduces the person of Jesus as the Word of God. Matthew and Luke choose to make use of the infancy narratives as their introduction to their gospels. In every case, these introductions came last, the final stage in completing the Good News. These also used the death and resurrection theology as their basis.

The infancy narratives, then, fall in the category of an introduction. They are like a prologue in a drama. They are like an overture to a symphony. They are like an introduction to a book. These narratives not only set the scene for the rest of the gospel story, but they are the gospel in miniature. Matthew and Luke are not only interested in introducing their gospels with these stories, but also to give a series of acknowledgements since they include a genealogy of Jesus' family tree. Gathering from all the gospels, one can see that the family background of Jesus was well known. Matthew and Luke had no intention of giving the genealogies and infancy narratives as information about Jesus' family, but they had another purpose. They wished to show that Jesus was both a product of human nature and also something above human nature at the same time. Jesus was no ordinary person and they wanted to state this very early in their gospels, thus the infancy narratives were recorded to do this.

The birth stories were written probably toward the end of the first century. These stories are anything but biography. They do not intend to relate historical facts in the sense that we today attach to history or facts. The Israeli writers of the New Testament period never recorded chronological, factual, or historical data as such. Their writings were filled with imagery and symbolism without any intent of deceiving, but rather of making an association of ideas that spoke the truth despite the lack of facts, figures, and order. Therefore, I repeat, the infancy narratives are not biography. It is rather the other way around, for the writers felt the need to narrate something about the birth of Jesus only long after he died and was buried. The infancy narratives are a reflection—a mirroring back of the resurrection stories. The first Christian communities began by celebrating only Easter—with the faith that the Lord was alive, and not dead. They slowly developed the Sunday celebration, which they called "little Easter." From that point they began gradually to think about and narrate a story of the beginning and his coming. Therefore, the infancy narratives are, properly speaking, Easter stories, but looked at in retrospect. Hence, there are all sorts of parallel images and symbolism between the Easter and Christmas stories (the angels, the light, the night, the often-repeated "do not fear," and many others). At the same time there are symbolic references to the Old Testament (the dreams of Joseph, the going to Egypt and the return, the star, the announcement of the birth by angels just as with Samson and Samuel). In short, both the

Easter and Christmas narratives are like two-way mirrors in which all sorts of things are reflected back and forth.

What did Matthew and Luke accomplish by including or even constructing these infancy narratives themselves? I suggest that Matthew and Luke were interested in giving Jesus a name. To name Jesus would make him live forever in our midst. The Jews struggled for centuries in finding a name for God. Now, they believed, God had come in this man, Jesus of Nazareth, and finally, they could name him. Why a name? What could this solve? A name is more than a word. A person's name is full of history. A person's name at once calls to mind facts and experiences, joy and sorrow, misunderstandings. When I speak the names of my friends, I am at once reminded of what I have in common with them, of what binds us together. People sometimes say of a dead person: "When I speak his (her) name, he (she) is there." Calling someone by his name is giving him the chance to become himself, addressing him as he is. You can humiliate a person, isolate her, and even dehumanize her if you never speak her name, but always make do with a nickname or some corruption of her real name or if you just call out to her, "hey, you."

Calling Jesus by a name—calling him, "Yeshua"—the Israelites call him Messiah; Isaiah calls him Wonder, Counselor; Matthew calls him son of Joseph, son of David, son of Abraham; Luke calls him son of Adam, son of God. There does not seem to be one name that captures this man "Jesus." The name "Jesus" brings to mind all people, all things, all meaning, all truth, all visions. The name "Jesus" stirs each individual in a different way. He is everything to everyone. Maybe this is what Matthew and Luke are trying to say. He is the Son of people. He belongs to all people, because all people can find themselves in him. Every man, woman, and child can discover their true identity in this man. We can find ourselves in him—the person he was and the life he lived. We can identify with him. We can live, because he lived for us. His life was like our own: A family tree, a name, childhood, the pain of growing, the pain of death. Then we too can remember him and name him and recommend him to each other as the living one.

Matthew and Luke are saying that the unnamable God has become a name in our midst.

Jesus becomes himself in people and God becomes human in Jesus.

10.
THE GOSPEL OF MARK

Reading: Mark 10:46-52

Traditionally, the author of this Gospel is identified with that John Mark whom the New Testament associates with St. Paul (Acts 12:25, 15:37-39; Col. 4:10; II Tim. 4:11; Philem. 24) and with St. Peter (Acts 12:12, I Pet. 5:13). Yet, we know today that the authors of all four Gospels are unknown. This Gospel was probably written around the year 75 CE and somewhere in the city of Rome. This Gospel is the oldest and shortest of the four, having only sixteen chapters and originally ending with chapter 16, verse 8. Anything you find printed in your Bibles after chapter 16, verse 8, are additions made at a later date by someone other than Mark. The reason for these additions was apparently to make Mark's Gospel more in line with the other three Gospels, which contained stories of appearances after the resurrection. Mark would never have added these verses since they violate the purpose of his Gospel. Also, the style of writing in these verses is not his, which is the clue that they were later additions.

On internal evidence, it is clear that this Gospel was written for non-Jewish Christians of pagan origin. There is little concern to show the connection of the Christian Gospel to the Old Testament, and, on the other hand, Mark takes great care to explain Jewish customs. For example during the crucifixion story we find: "And when evening had come, since it was the Day of Preparation, that is, the day before the Sabbath..." (Mark 15:42). The point being that if his readers were Jewish, Mark would not have to explain that the "Day of Preparation" was the "day before the Sabbath." A Jewish reader would have known this. You also notice that he translates Hebrew words for his readers such as in the reading above: "Bartimaeus, a blind man, the son of Timaeus" (Mark 10:46). Again, a Jewish reader would not need this translation. Therefore, we can conclude that this Gospel was written for non-Jewish Christians.

The main theological structure of the Gospel falls into two parts: First, the Mystery of the Messiah; secondly, the Mystery of the Son of God. In the first part (the Mystery of the Messiah) the emphasis is on the miracles of Jesus. There is little teaching as Jesus tries to conceal his messiahship, although he rebukes his disciples for their inability to understand who he is. In the second part (the Mystery of the Son of God) miracles are rare and the emphasis falls more on the teaching of Jesus. This teaching is directed mostly to his disciples as he continues to conceal his messiahship to outsiders who could easily misinterpret it. This is always indicated by a similar phrase throughout the Gospel: "Then he gave them strict orders not to tell anyone about him" (Mark 8:30).

This great secret and mystery is maintained from the beginning to the end of this Gospel by Mark, even to the very last line, which says: "They made their way out and fled from the tomb bewildered and trembling; and because of their great fear, they said nothing to anyone" (Mark 16:8). In the first part of the Gospel, Jesus preaches to all of Israel without success. In the second part, he reveals his identity to his disciples without any greater success. The revelation of who Jesus is takes place at the moment of his death—when a pagan centurion (a non-Jew) boldly proclaims, "Truly, this is the Son of God" (Mark 15:39).

The entire Gospel is set up to produce a faith response on the part of the reader or audience. Mark's intention is to make the nonbeliever believe and the believer to believe more. Therefore, he avoids a faith response on the part of the characters in the Gospel proper. Israel does not believe. His disciples do not understand him; but, you, the reader, you are led step by step to faith.

Mark only describes faith responses in his characters when he wants to teach his audience and readers what they should be doing (in other words, what you and I who read this Gospel must do). That is why in the passages from Mark's Gospel above, Jesus says to the blind Bartimaeus: "Be on your way! Your **faith** has healed you" (Mark 10:52).

The blind man believes—and he is cured! It is not the miracle that causes cures—no—it is the **faith** of people. Therefore, Mark does not wish you to believe because he wrote his Gospel…BUT, if you are a believer first, then the Gospel will have meaning for you. Then you will be healed. Then **you** will see!

11.
WISDOM IN THE GOSPEL OF MARK

Reading: Mark 10:35-45

The Gospel of Mark (being the first Gospel) was the major source for the Gospels of Luke and Matthew. If Mark's was the first Gospel—then he had no Gospel tradition to follow. He was his own boss. Nobody got the first word. No one took away his clout. He held the punch line. And he used it well. Throughout this Gospel, there is this poignant secret, which is alluded to over and over, exposed only slightly here and there—all to the dismay of Jesus' Jewish audience. At the climax of the Gospel—a Gentile—unmasks the secret and lays it bare!

The moment one discovers that secret will be a moment of WISDOM. Faith is the condition for Wisdom in this Gospel—a faith that will help you endure whatever comes along. Faith is the patience it takes—but Mark doesn't mind if it's an impatient patience, like a child who asks over and over again, "Are we there yet?"

This Gospel is filled with many Wisdom teachings. Wisdom is an old Hebrew idea of elusive learning. Every time you hear a Wisdom teaching, you are usually puzzled by it, but at the same time you really know what it's saying. Let me give you a few examples from Mark that will help you better understand what I mean:

4:25 "To those who have, more will be given; from those who have not, what little they have will be taken away."

7:15 "Nothing that enters a person from outside can make him impure; that which comes out of him, and only that, constitutes impurity."

8:35 "Whoever would preserve his life will lose it, but whoever loses his life for my sake and the gospel's will preserve it."

9:43-50 "If your hand is your difficulty, cut it off...If your foot is your undoing, cut it off...If your eye is your downfall, tear it out...(Better for you to enter the Kingdom of God with one than Gehenna with two)."

10:15 "Whoever does not accept the reign of God like a little child shall not take part in it."

10:25 "It is easier for a camel to pass through a needle's eye than for a rich person to enter the Kingdom of God."

10:31 "Many who are first shall come last, and the last shall come first."

10:43-44 "Anyone among you who aspires to greatness must serve the rest; whoever wants to rank first among you must serve the needs of all."

Notice the paradoxes—the opposites—the shock value—and now you see how Jesus taught in the Gospel of Mark. But in this Gospel no one ever seems to understand him. And now we are back to the secret Mark keeps all throughout his Gospel—and this too is a Wisdom way of teaching—let everyone know there's a secret, and keep revealing it without anyone ever getting it. The secret lies in the dead Jesus and not the risen Jesus. If one can come to faith in the dead Jesus, for Mark, this is a more authentic faith. Believing in miracles, wonders, teaching, etc. is no faith for Mark. Faith in this Gospel is at the moment of death, your lowest moment, when you are down, giving all and receiving nothing in return.

Thus, the passage above is within this context of Mark's concept of authentic faith:

—Authentic service is the result of authentic faith.

—Authentic faith is proven by pain, death, sorrow, suffering, sacrifice.

—It's too easy to say you believe when things are going well.

Can you drink the cup that Jesus drank and still have faith?

—Even more—can you believe in a God who drinks the cup
that we have to drink?

—Is your faith in the dead Jesus or the risen Jesus in glory?

—The kind of service you give is the answer to that question!

—The kind of service that is proof of an authentic faith in Jesus
is service till it kills you!

12.
THE BEGINNING OF THE GOSPEL OF MARK

Reading: Mark 1:1-8

The Gospel of Mark: An adventure in faith, an exercise of wisdom, a story of Jesus, a Gentile perspective, a multitude of theologies, an original piece of literature, written by a second-generation Christian, a gospel of contrasts, a gospel with a secret, a gospel of paradox, a work of art, with unity of purpose.

You just read the first eight verses of the first chapter. What did you see? You saw a lot more than your eyes conveyed. This Gospel will reprimand you over and over again for having ears, but not hearing—for having eyes, but not seeing!

The "secret" of this Gospel was revealed already—did you perceive it? The how of this secret is yet to be revealed. The "faith" demanded by this Gospel is already being tested—did you notice? The first "paradoxes" of this Gospel were put forth—did you feel them? I think we better reexamine those first eight verses.

(Read Mark 1:1-8 again.)

Verse one refers to this work as Good News or Gospel. Mark is the only Evangelist who entitles his work "Gospel." For Mark, this is Good News and Good News is salvation. This Good News is also equated with Jesus and Jesus is equated with Christ. Jesus **proclaims** the Good News and Jesus **is** the Good News. This proclamation is what makes salvation present in the world.

Verses two to eight link the Old Testament and New Testament in the person of John the Baptist with a quote from Isaiah.

Notice how Mark creates various contrasts and paradoxes with a wisdom motif: Jesus—Christ

Old Testament—New Testament

Isaiah—John the Baptist

John the Baptist—Jesus

John the Baptist—Elijah

Water—Spirit

Sin—Forgiveness

Conclusion: The moment of wisdom for you will be that moment when your ears do hear and your eyes do see for the first time what Mark means by calling this a Gospel or Good News!

13.
A MIRACLE IN MARK'S GOSPEL

Reading: Mark 1:21-28

As we begin to take a look at this passage, keep in mind all the things you already know about the Gospel of Mark. Also note that it is Chapter 1, verses 21 to 28.

Did you notice that the unclean spirit knows who Jesus is while the witnesses to this miracle (the onlookers) have to ask, "What does this mean?" Mark does this on purpose! And he will continue to do this all throughout the Gospel. Mark contrasts the *likely* with the *unlikely*. The most unlikely to know who Jesus is or have any faith in Jesus would be an evil spirit—yet that evil spirit says, "I know who you are—the Holy One of God!" Notice then that Jesus rebukes the evil spirit by telling it to be quiet—in other words, Mark is strengthening the contrast by trying to keep the likely ones from finding out who Jesus is! The most likely to believe in and know Jesus would be the witnesses or onlookers in the synagogue. In contrast to the evil spirit, these witnesses have to ask: "WHAT DOES THIS MEAN?"

Mark is telling us, the readers, that seeing a miracle is not a good basis for faith. All the witnesses of the miracle still had questions about who Jesus was. Not even witnessing one of his miracles and hearing his authoritative teaching convinced them of who he was. Mark is saying that faith in Jesus is not to be built on his miracles and teaching—and that's part of the secret—knowing the secret will take a much greater faith than one built on outward signs and proof.

For the Evangelist, Mark, what constitutes faith in Jesus is not flashy miracles, not learned teaching, not even Mark's Gospel. What constitutes **real faith** in Jesus is this Gospel's secret, kept for the moment when only the **true believer** will clearly understand!

Something for you to think about: In Mark's eyes, what is real faith and who is the true believer?

14.
THE KINGDOM OF GOD IN MARK'S GOSPEL

Readings: Ezekiel 17:22-24 Mark 4:26-34

When Jesus looked for images to describe the Kingdom of God he looked for images in the Hebrew Scripture that described Israel.

As most Jews of his day, he prophesied that Israel would become the Kingdom of God, that the Kingdom of God would be here on earth and take root in Israel. In fact, according to Ezekiel, it was already rooted in Israel. Jesus knew this and so spoke of this root or seed as waiting to sprout at any moment.

In Mark's Gospel, Jesus came to proclaim the Kingdom of God! He came to remind Israel that she was the garden in which this seed was planted and she needed to care and nurture this garden faithfully so that the Kingdom could flower and bloom, and that someday all nations of the earth would come and nest in her branches.

Ironically enough—through Christianity—all nations have come to nest in the branches of Israel. Through the Jew, Yeshua, Jesus, the Gentiles have been grafted on the tree and share the root and seed which is to become the Kingdom of God.

And so, applying everything you already know about the Gospel of Mark, let's interpret these parables about the kingdom of God. The "seed" is faith. The "soil" is believers. The "ready crop" are the martyrs for the faith. The "mustard seed" is faith (almost unseen).

Mark is saying that faith produces growth. Ezekiel and Mark together are saying that God is the sower of the seed, the planter of faith, the sower of a people of faith. Israel is the kingdom by virtue of being a people of faith.

And finally, Mark makes it very clear that true believers would understand all this. Weak believers will need explanations. Mark is hinting at another problem, that of *private* versus *communal* interpretation of the parables. Only Jesus can interpret the parables, and he has passed that power on to his Church. The Christian Church, "now planted on the mountain heights of Israel," will, along with Israel, be the authentic interpreters of God's word in the parables of this Gospel.

The Good News or Gospel for Mark is that **Jesus** is the proclaimer and the bringer of the kingdom of God.

15.
A STORY IN MARK'S GOSPEL

Reading: Mark 4:35-41

Every story about Jesus in the New Testament is a story about his death and resurrection. The death and resurrection of Jesus were the *kerygma* or core of the Good News proclaimed by the early Church—the original mystery that sparked Christianity—the central act of redemption and salvation revealed by Jesus. Therefore, every story about Jesus in the New Testament is a story about his death and resurrection.

Let's look at the story above in Mark's Gospel to see this. Here are the biblical images and symbols Mark uses in this story: The sea = life; the boat = the church; the storm = life's problems, conflicts and disappointments; the sleeping Jesus = the dead or absent Jesus; the awakened Jesus = the risen Christ; the complaining disciples = weak believers.

Also look at how Mark is able to symbolically compare the Old and New testaments: In the OT only God controls the waters and all nature—in the NT Jesus controls the waters and is therefore from God; in the OT only God has power over life—in the NT Jesus has power over life and therefore is identified with God; in the OT faith is put in God—in the NT faith in Jesus is faith in God. Take note that Jesus was in the stern (in control) even as he slept.

Why are the disciples weak believers? Because they have no faith in the dead or absent Jesus. They need resurrection as a sign to spark their faith. Jesus awakens (or rises), only to rebuke both them and the storm. He calms the storm which is their lack of faith.

True believers would be able to allow Jesus to sleep, while still placing faith in this sleeping (dead and absent) Jesus. For the Evangelist, Mark, then, the sleeping Jesus is the object of faith for the true believer. The awakened Jesus gives only a reprimand to the weak believers.

In this Gospel, all the miraculous events and teachings (including the resurrection), are met with no faith response—only fear, silence, or misunderstanding. Notice: "Who can this be that the wind and the sea obey him?" (4:41). It is only at the death of Jesus where the full response of faith can be made. If you cannot identify Jesus with his death—how could you identify yourself as his follower—since your identity as a Christian is one who is expected to lose your own life?

Jesus teaches wisdom: To save your life, you must lose it!

It is clear from this story that the Church Mark was addressing was a Church who was struggling with their faith in an absent Jesus. Jesus' crucifixion was a stormy experience in the life of the early church. They longed to experience the resurrection as their ancestors did. They longed for his second coming as their ancestors promised. Mark was trying to help the Church of his day cope with the sleeping (or dead or absent) Jesus, and remain faithful to their situation and not waver in the face of life's turbulences (a turbulence that was really created by their lack of faith).

Mark suggests to his Church, that a church that has faith only when things are calm and going well is not a church with genuine faith. Faith in the awakened or resurrected Jesus is easy. Faith in the sleeping or crucified Lord is genuine. In the entire Gospel, only one person exhibits that kind of faith. Who it is and when it will occur will be significant for Mark's purpose.

(And now read Mark 8:34-38 as a fitting conclusion to this story.)

16.
A LESSON IN MARK'S GOSPEL

Readings: Mark 10:13-16, and then Mark 9:36-37

Why are we just as surprised today as those who first heard Jesus speak that baffling paradox? What is it that keeps us from taking Jesus seriously about the words we just read? Why do we always want to explain the thought away—that an adult should become a child!

Is it because we do not always think of children as fully human, equal to ourselves, in need of learning and education, needing to be told, to be subordinate to our authority, an object of our wants and desires, someone we turn into "another me"? For most of us, childhood is a stage to be condescendingly remembered, a state behind us, when "I didn't know anything." The world revolves around adults. And we adults are people who know what we want and have hands to make and break.

But, when we listen to the Gospel of Mark, we begin to approach the dawn of realization. We cannot escape the suspicion that somehow, paradoxically, things have turned: You are not a child to become an adult—You are an adult to become a child! The "child" is not only our origin, but also our final point, the vision! The "child" is the light in the distance, something to be grown into—our future!

And we, who are supposed to be so wise, ask: "How?" "How do we do this?" Well, perhaps in this way...

The "child" in our midst is much more than a small person having to grow up. Somehow, the child is the best we have—the best of ourselves—our greatest treasure. When calamity strikes, children are always saved first. If the child is lost, everything is lost. No one can pass the child by. If children are hungry or killed, we are horrified. The child opens our eyes—is so authentically human that one can recognize oneself in the child. The child strips us of everything we have built up around ourselves. The child is the one with the questions and not the answers. The child brings you back to your most proper essence; takes you by the hand to lead you to what *you also* want to be: defenseless, innocent, not having all the answers, open, a dreamer, without pomp, without weapons, and especially wise. The child in us is the primitive essence that we have buried deeply behind all kinds of worries, anxieties, conventions, aggressions, and other foolishness.

The Gospel of Mark is the story of how it is possible to return to our essence, of how it is possible to uncover or reveal once again the child in each of us. When God created Adam and Eve, they were naked and not ashamed. Who is the only one you know in our world, who can run around naked and unashamed? A child, of course! The moment Adam and Eve sinned, was the moment their nakedness shamed them. Sin had wiped away their innocence, their childhood, and made them into adults. When we sin, we are no longer children! It is no wonder, then, that God sent a child into our world to save us from sin—for only a child is without sin.

Mark's Gospel is the story of a *child* coming to save adults. It is the story of *light* coming to brighten the darkness of sin. This is the story of *wisdom* coming to disperse the foolish. Jesus came into our world as a child, a light, wisdom—and the paradox continues: You not only have to be a child to enter the kingdom, you must also be a child to enter this world. The child, then, is the turning point of wisdom, the dawn! The child is the beginning and the end!

Perhaps that's why the elderly become like children. It's the only way to come and go between heaven and earth, between death and life, between darkness and light, between the human and divine. Perhaps that's why we have always referred to old age as wisdom.

The Gospel calls all of us to wisdom! The Gospel calls all of us to the kingdom! If we are to enter the kingdom, to know the One who sent Jesus, then we must be born again and again. For to be a human being is to howl throughout life from the pains of birth. To be born again is to welcome back the child in you. And to welcome the child in you is to welcome—God!

17.
AN EXAMPLE OF FAITH IN MARK'S GOSPEL

Reading: Mark 12:38-44

The term "poor" had a different meaning in the time of Jesus and in that culture than it does in our American culture today. When we Americans think of "poor," we immediately think economics, lack of money, food, shelter, and clothing.

In first-century Israel and even in parts of today's Mediterranean culture, the term "poor" was not used to describe one's economic status.

In the Bible, the "poor" were the widows and orphans; not because a widow or orphan had little or no money—in fact, many widows were financially well-off—but because widows and orphans had lost their source of identity.

In a culture like the Bible, where a man's identity stemmed from his father (son of Jesse, son of Judah, son of Abraham), an orphan had no identity since he had no parents.

In a culture like the Bible, where a woman's identity stemmed from her husband (all women were expected to be married), a widow had no identity since she had no husband.

In the Bible, then, one is poor when one has no identity. The poor were the widows and orphans.

In the Gospel of Mark, Jesus gives a certain widow her identity. The widow in this Gospel gets her identity from Jesus. Jesus points her out as a woman of great faith. Her story is written down. She is known to all of us. Paradoxically, this is one Mediterranean widow whose identity is known all over the world.

The widow's identity is a woman of great faith. In a Gospel like Mark's, you would expect that she would be an example of faith. And, of course, we all know why...

Mark (as is his custom in almost every story) contrasts the person of faith with those who lack faith. In this story, the scribes and the wealthy

REVEREND ROBERT E. ALBRIGHT

are those who are lacking in faith, who are really "the poor" while the widow is identified for all time as the one with faith. Why?

Because faith is something you have when you have nothing else. Faith is giving what little you have to give. Faith is giving when you have nothing to give. Faith, then, becomes the gift itself. The widow's penny was not her gift. Her gift was her steadfast faith—her example of faith—in contrast to the scribes, and as a model for the disciples.

The author of this Gospel, Mark, is constantly challenging the faith of his readers. At this point in the Gospel, his ideal model of faith—the widow—is acknowledged by Jesus to his disciples. Mark is calling on every reader of this Gospel to that kind of faith the widow had.

Do **you** have that kind of faith?!?

18.
THE END OF THE WORLD

Readings: Daniel 12:1-3 Mark 13:24-32

The end of the world! What will it be like? When will it happen? Will it be as you heard described in the Scripture above? Do you believe the world will end? Or do you scoff and laugh at the thought?

Let us first look into the Scripture to see what it tells us. The prophet Daniel envisions a future time when all people will be liberated from the present human condition. There's a hint at what will determine this liberation—justice, wisdom, living a good life, and helping others to do the same. Every prophet of the Old Testament harbored this vision of the future; every prophet dreamed the dream of peace, a new city, a new Jerusalem, a place where justice and peace would reign. Even the name, *Yerushalayim* had emotional overtones. One hears in it the Hebrew words *shalom* meaning "peace" or *yishlayu* meaning "rest" or *shalwah* meaning "happiness." And so Jerusalem became the symbol of the future peace, the future city without death or darkness.

In the New Testament we find the same vision and desires, but colored by another hope: the hope that this new city would be imminent. From Mark's Gospel, we can see that Jesus promised to come again, and soon—at least the early Christians believed this. Notice this verse: "I assure you, *this generation* will not pass away until all these things take place. The heavens and the earth will pass away, but my words will not" (Mark 13:30-31).

Almost every chapter and verse of the New Testament is shaded by this belief that Jesus would come at any moment. It was almost one hundred years before the Church gave up on believing that the second coming was imminent, but never gave up believing that someday in the future there would be a new heaven and a new earth, where justice will prevail. And very early in our Christian tradition a liturgical season was established to express this desire, this vision—we call it Advent (celebrated for four weeks in preparation for Christmas).

By the end of the first century, when the Gospel of John was being written, he had already given up the idea of the imminent second coming—for we can find no story of the end of the world in his Gospel nor any reference to it, as we do in Mark or Matthew or Luke. Rather, it is John who gives us a new insight that the kingdom, the new creation, became imminent and was begun in Jesus and is continued in us here and now. For John, it is not some future reality only that will come with some cataclysmic intervention, but because of Jesus it is real here and now. Even in Luke's Gospel where one does find a story about the end of the world, we also find Jesus saying, "The Kingdom of God is within you" (Luke 17:20-21).

There are different theologies in the Scripture—some ask us to set our sights on the things above and others ask us to set our sights on this earth. It is in the commandment of love where Jesus brings these two sights together—for to love our neighbor **is** to love God—for to live for others **is** salvation—for to live a good life **is** building the Kingdom— and notice well, in Mark's Gospel we learn that when we can love one another, not only the old earth, but even our old ideas of heaven will pass away and there will be a new earth and a new heaven.

What does this all mean? We may never know! But there is one thing we do know—and that is: that you and I are alive! That we have been given life! That we believe in life, that we live over and over again the life of the man from Nazareth who was killed for no reason by other people, and that this is the life lived by God. And because God came among us in Jesus, we have learned that *this* intervention was cataclysmic enough—enough for some, too much for others, not enough for some, but felt by all Christians—Christians who are asked to live in spite of death; Christians who are asked to love in spite of hate; Christians who are asked to, "Come, follow me" (Matt. 9:9) "and I will raise you up on the last day" (John 6:54).

We are not a people who live out of fear, the fear of the world ending or a last judgment. We are people called to live life to the fullest, out of love, and know that when we can work out our problems and solve our conflicts, when we can come to see the beauty of one another's diversity, when we welcome every human being as a brother or sister, then the kingdom will come.

The kingdom is not a place or a state of affairs! The kingdom is God surprising us here and there, when and where we least expect it—coming to us in people and events we least expect. God's ever-present, surprise-involvement in time and history is the Kingdom of God. So, be like a child—enjoy the surprises—wait for them eagerly—welcome them with laughter—and remember the greatest surprise of all: Whoever accepts the Kingdom of God like a child shall enter into it (cf. Mark 10:15).

19.
THE PASSION ACCORDING TO MARK

Reading: Mark 14:1-15:47

Well, there it is—the Passion According to Saint Mark. The secret in Mark's Gospel has been revealed! The climax in a Gospel where no one seems to have an adequate faith in Jesus is when the one least expected reveals this well-kept secret!

Who was it? And what is the secret?

All through Mark's Gospel, the "faithful" do not recognize anything. What a paradox! Mark tells us that people who are "faithful" remain faithful only to what they can see and prove (miracles, happenings, events, etc.).

Who could see anything but death, loss, and disappointment in the crucifixion?!

Yet, one man did recognize something. In contrast to everyone else present on Golgotha, the Roman centurion, the one keeping guard, a Gentile, a pagan, an unbeliever, without any provocation, reveals the secret of who Jesus is and the secret of the true believer. He calls Jesus, "the Son of God"—"Clearly," he says! Yet, it is not clear to anyone else, not even the women who ministered to Jesus (Mary Magdalene, another Mary, and Salome). Why is it "clear" to this unlikely candidate? To this unnamed soldier? He has no reason to believe. No one taught him or raised him to believe. No one did anything extraordinary to provoke belief on his part. Here, Mark, the author of this Gospel is giving us the central and greatest message of his whole Gospel: This moment is the only moment of real faith. All other moments are too easy, too obvious, too deceiving, too provocative. Only this moment is the true one! The moment one has no reason to believe is the moment of greatest faith.

Moments where provocation comes from the outside can be deceiving. A miracle could be magic. Faith does not come by provocation. Faith comes by recognition. And recognition comes from within.

With his physical eyes, the centurion saw a prisoner die. With recognition, he saw beyond the fact of death, beyond the death of a slave on a cross, to seeing that this was not death, but life, and that this was no slave, but the Son of God.

In this Gospel, the Roman centurion, then, is the symbol of all true believers. And what a symbol, especially for Mark's audience, who probably were right in the heart of Rome itself! The death of Jesus, then, is the center of all faith in Jesus. The true believer is one who recognizes often what others do not. Recognizing is believing! Recognition is *our* choice, not someone else's. Recognition is never forced on us. Recognition is *our* free choice. Because recognition is "seeing" what we cannot "see" with our eyes! Faith doesn't come by closing your eyes and trying hard to believe. Faith comes when you least expect it. You simply have to wait and see! And as Mark told you earlier in his Gospel: You have to "be on guard" (Mark 13:23, 32-37).

There are some people who are struggling with whether Jesus is God or not—some are struggling with a decision to enter the Church—some struggle with commitment to the Church—whether to be confirmed or not, whether to stay in the Church or not. These are moments of faith. Recognize them for what they really are. Don't abandon your post. Wait it out.

And so, I can only leave you with Mark's injunction: "Be on guard." For like the unnamed soldier who was on guard at the cross, faith will come to you when you least expect it—but only if you are "on guard."

20.
EASTER IN MARK'S GOSPEL

Reading: Mark 16:1-8

Well, there it is—that bleak ending to a story without rapture or joy..."He is risen"...Again, as always in this Gospel, no recognition...No one takes up the refrain "He is risen"—no one sings "Alleluia"—no one even knows what that means—no recognition—only fear and bewilderment. Again, the author of this shortest Gospel is telling us that not even the appearance of an angel can give us faith—not even an earth-shattering experience like an empty tomb can stir faith—not even the writing of this Gospel can give you faith. Faith comes with recognition! Recognition comes from within! These same "faithful" women were present on Golgotha and now at the empty tomb and have yet to recognize anything! Instead, they run away and say nothing. When you have no faith—there is nothing to tell.

Unlike these women, we who read this story have the advantage of the rest of the Bible. Every story in the Bible is a story in which someone has recognized something. These are stories of faith! With every story we read, we are hearing someone else's faith. Hopefully, it is our faith too! With every story we read, we are experiencing someone else's recognition. Hopefully, we too can recognize it!

The word for *Easter* in most languages is "Passover" or a derivative of it: *Pasqua, Pasch, Paschalis, Paschal candle, Paschal moon.* Even the Germanic word *Easter* means to "rise in the east" (Oster, Ooster). To "Easter" not only means to rise, but to "pass over," as the sun and the stars do from east to west.

Easter, then, is a time when we tell stories about the God who has passed through our lives, about people who have passed through life itself: The earth passed from darkness to light (Gen. 1:1). People passed from no existence to life (Gen. 1:27). Israel passed through the sea from slavery to freedom (Exod. 12:31). Jesus passed from death to resurrection

(Mark 16:6). These stories tell us that as God passed through the lives of Israel by making a covenant with them through Moses and the Law, so too did that same God pass by in the person of Jesus, another Jewish man, to give us non-Jews the same mercy and love by making us partakers and sharers in that same covenant.

Our mothers and fathers, the first Christians, were the ones who "recognized" this connection and have passed this faith on to us in the writings of the Gospels.

So, once again, in the light of these many stories, some of us find ourselves shivering naked in a brand new world, others of us find ourselves cowering before a raging sea, some of us find ourselves cringing at the foot of the cross, others of us find ourselves gaping at an empty tomb.

All of us, however, are faced with the same question: what does all this mean? Those of us who "recognize" what happened in these stories will go out and tell everyone about it. Those of us who do not recognize what happened in these stories will go away bewildered and tell no one anything. The saving grace for both those who *do* recognize and those who *do not* is that you can always open the Bible and read these stories again and again and again...until...?!

21.
THE GOSPEL OF MATTHEW

Readings: Isaiah 11:1-10 Romans 15:4-9 Matthew 3:1-12

Who was Matthew? When did he live? Why did he write a Gospel? What is his unique message?

"Matthew" is not the person we generally think of when we hear that name. He is not one of Jesus' twelve Apostles (one of whom was named "Matthew"). Remember, there were numerous Jews in the first century with the name "Matthew." But, besides this, there are indications that this particular "Matthew" who wrote the Gospel according to Matthew, did not live at the time of Jesus. In fact, we can locate this Gospel in place and time with enough surety to say that its author did not know Jesus personally nor live in the time and place of Jesus of Nazareth.

Jesus lived in Palestine somewhere between the years 1 and 33 of the Common Era. Matthew lived in Syria somewhere between the years 60 and 90 of the Common Era. Matthew was a second-generation Christian—most likely a Jew—who grew up in the Jewish/Christian community at Antioch, the capital city of Syria. He wrote his Gospel somewhere around the year 80 of the Common Era—and from all internal evidence of this Gospel, the audience for whom it was written was a predominantly Jewish/Christian one, with some Gentile converts.

The Gospel of Matthew is the most Jewish of all the four Gospels. The audience for whom it is intended is clearly Jewish, and the author himself displays enough familiarity with the Hebrew Scriptures that we presume he was Jewish also. Given this Jewish context, then, we begin to discover in this Gospel certain themes that surround and impact the Jewish audience for whom it was intended. As I just mentioned, Matthew's audience was predominantly a Jewish-Christian community with some Gentile converts, living in Antioch around the year 80 of the Common Era.

Therefore, the themes Matthew chooses for his Gospel are Jewish ones—meaningful to those whose lives were governed by the Torah (The Law) and the writings of the Prophets—the Law and the Prophets—both of which are the basis for all the Hebrew Scriptures.

Matthew's Gospel has five major themes:

1. Jesus as the long-awaited Messiah.
2. Jesus as the fulfillment of the Law and the Prophets.
3. The Church as the extension of Israel.
4. The entry of the Gentiles into the Church as God's Plan.
5. Jesus as the Emmanuel, God with us.

For Matthew, John the Baptist comes on the scene to fulfill what was spoken by the prophet Isaiah, and this is the prophet who bridges the old and the new, the Torah and Jesus, Israel and the Church, the Jewish covenant and the Christian covenant. Even John the Baptist is fulfilling the prophecies as he becomes the voice of the precursor or messenger or herald who points to Jesus as the total fulfillment of all Israel's expectations. He says, "One who will follow me is more powerful than I" (Matt. 3:11).

A second theme is hinted at in the Gospel when John tells the Jews, "I tell you, God can raise up children to Abraham from these very stones" (Matt. 3:9). This is a clear reference to the Gentiles. Remember the promise God makes to Abraham in Genesis: "And in your descendants all the nations of the earth shall find blessing" (Gen. 22:18). *All the nations of the earth* are the Gentiles. Gentiles will find blessing through Abraham's descendants. Isaiah's prophecy is also fulfilled: "On that day, the root of Jesse, set up as a signal to the nations (Nes Ammim), the Gentiles shall seek out" (Isa. 11:10). Matthew sees Jesus as the descendant of Abraham through whom all the Gentiles can inherit God's blessing.

The Gospel of Matthew, then, is "good news" for both Jews and Gentiles, the old and the new. The "good news" for the Gentiles is that we are now part of God's covenant—we share God's care and goodness in the same intimate fashion as Israel had for hundreds of years. The "good news" for the Jews is that God kept the promise and fulfilled a prophecy—one of their descendants fulfilled what God promised long ago to Abraham and prophesied through Isaiah—a promise fulfilled, a promise realized in the Gentile-Christian world. Through the Jew, Jesus, Gentiles now share the covenant.

Besides these themes, Matthew's Gospel is fraught with tension/ victims/violence from beginning to end. Tension is the keynote of Matthew's Gospel. It is the thread that holds this Gospel together from beginning to end. Unlike the Gospel of Luke with its aura of peace and reconciliation, the Gospel of Matthew will keep you on the edge of your seat from start to finish.

The tension starts with questionable women in Jesus' genealogy; then moves to Joseph wanting to divorce his questionably pregnant wife, Mary; then to Herod trying to kill Jesus by destroying the innocent boys in Bethlehem; then look at the tension in Jesus' adult life—being tempted by Satan in the desert, always at odds with his fellow Jews, calling the Pharisees names; tensions between Jews and Gentiles, between Galilee and Jerusalem; the ultimate tension of the cross; the final moments of tension in the stolen body accusation, and that some disciples still doubted Jesus after the resurrection!

And how can we not forget about how Matthew treats the end of the world story: Some will be taken and some will be left—be on guard— stay awake—you know neither the hour nor the day!

What does all of this suggest? That this Gospel was written in a time of high tension—tension between Jews who had become Christians and Jews who were expelling Christian Jews from their synagogue in Antioch. This caused further tension within Matthew's community since many of his fellow Jewish Christians began to lose faith in Jesus as a result of this persecution.

Matthew lifts his pen to address the tensions in his community in the year 80 with his story of the life of Jesus in the year 30. Matthew writes his Gospel with such force and inspiration that every member of his complex community could see him or herself in the Jesus story. Matthew presents Jesus as someone who still speaks to this world and its problems fifty years after his death and resurrection. Matthew quells the tensions of the squalls and storms within his community with the story of Jesus who calms the wind and walks on the disturbed waters. Matthew answers the burning questions about Gentiles entering the Church with parable after parable in the mouth of Jesus and in the ingenious story of the astrologer magi Gentiles who seek the newborn savior. Matthew answers the doubters among his fellow Christians by reminding them of Peter who sank beneath the water and denied Jesus three times, of

Judas who handed Jesus over, and of all the disciples who left him and fled. Finally, Matthew eases the tensions of his fellow Christians with his ultimate message that Jesus is always with them—in this Gospel he is Emmanuel, God with us—when two or three are gathered in his name, he is there in their midst—and as these Jewish disciples go out into all the world preaching and making Gentile disciples of all nations, Jesus reminds them, "I am with you until the end of time" (Matt. 28:20).

22.
THE SERMON ON THE MOUNT IN MATTHEW'S GOSPEL

Readings: Sirach 15:15-20 I Corinthians 2:6-10 Matthew 5:17-37

Matthew has obviously constructed this part of his Gospel as a synthesis or summary of all the teachings of Jesus. In order for his readers to see the message of Jesus more clearly, Matthew organizes and collects the teachings of Jesus into what we have come to call "the Sermon on the Mount" (chapters 5, 6, & 7).

But why does Matthew place Jesus on a mountain? If you recall, in Luke's Gospel, Jesus speaks the Beatitudes at the foot of a mountain along the seashore. What is Matthew's purpose for placing Jesus on a mountain to deliver this sermon?

To respond to this query will lead us to discover one of the overriding themes of Matthew's Gospel. From the internal structure of this Gospel, we can see that it was definitely written for a Jewish audience—a Jewish audience who had become Christian. A giveaway of this discovery is Matthew's constant quoting of the Old Testament. Only a Jewish audience could benefit from such a style of writing.

In connection with this, then, Matthew sets out to use many Old Testament themes in his treatment of Jesus. Why? Because Jews would better understand who Jesus is if they viewed him in light of the Old Testament, which they knew and understood so well.

The greatest character in all the Old Testament pages for the Jews was Moses. Matthew, obviously a Jew himself, knew this, and consequently creates a theme for his Gospel whereby he presents Jesus as *another Moses*!

Now we begin to see why Matthew places Jesus on a mountain when he delivers this famous sermon. In the Old Testament Moses received the Law from God on Mount Sinai. Therefore, to enhance this theme of Jesus as another Moses, Matthew places this incident on a mountain to recall Sinai.

All through this New Testament account of Matthew's, there is an attempt on Matthew's part to equate Jesus with Moses, to bring together the Old Law and the New Law, to make a connection between the Old Testament and the New Testament, between the God of the Old Testament and the God of the New Testament. Notice what Jesus says: He comes to *fulfill* the Law; the Law says no murder, Jesus says don't even get angry; the Law says no adultery, Jesus says don't even look lustfully at another person; the Law says go bring your gift to the altar, Jesus says don't do that unless you are first reconciled with your brothers and sisters.

And so, in the Sermon on the Mount we have a *fulfillment* of the Law, and that is a New Testament. Jesus fulfills the Law by protecting it from transgression. He builds a moral wall around each commandment. To ensure that a commandment is not broken, he suggests any prior action that would lead to breaking the commandment not even be taken. For example: To prevent breaking the Law not to murder, Jesus suggests not even to get angry. Anger leads to murder. Murder is forbidden in the covenant. One keeps further away from murder by trying to curb anger. If you take care of your anger, there will never be murder!

Another example for married couples: Let your "Yes" mean "Yes" and your "No" mean "No." In other words—if you keep your vows, there will be no need to divorce; if you do not divorce, you will not violate the commandment forbidding adultery. Again, Jesus is building a moral wall around the commandment to ensure that it not be broken. That's the fulfillment of the Law! That's the New Testament! Matthew is not suggesting Jesus is better than Moses or that the New Law is better than the Old. On the contrary—Matthew is saying they are complementary to each other. Only then could he truly evangelize his brother and sister Jews.

Matthew is very clever. He knows his audience. He plays to his audience. He writes for his audience. He did not write his Gospel for you and me. We are not Jews. We may never really understand fully the impact of Matthew's Gospel, and that is not his fault. We are not Jews or of Jewish descent. We do not live in the world in which this Gospel was written. We do not understand the times and troubles of the early Christians. We are a scientific and technological society. Matthew's audience was a poetic and close-to-nature people. Authors like Matthew never wrote for a literal-minded audience, but in images and symbolic language. We cannot even fathom many of these images and symbols, because we are so literal, so concrete, so exact, so factual.

Jesus most likely never spoke these words all at the same time standing on a mountain. Our cultural judgment is to take literally these chapters we read in the Scripture. Yet, if you are willing to go beyond the written word to scholarly interpretation and study, you begin to see the intention of the author, you begin to hear the message, you begin to know Jesus, you begin to believe!

If your present faith is the result of taking the Scripture literally, then you probably do not know the *real* Jesus at all!

23.
A PARABLE IN MATTHEW'S GOSPEL

Reading: Matthew 13:1-23

Jesus tells a parable—Matthew interprets it. Jesus lived approximately 30-33 CE—Matthew lived approximately 80 CE. Jesus lived before the *diaspora*—Matthew lived in the *diaspora*. (The *diaspora* began with the Jewish revolt against the Romans in 70 CE. When the Romans finally conquered the Jews after two years, in retaliation they murdered the priests, destroyed Jerusalem and the temple, and then *dispersed* the Jews throughout the Roman Empire, no longer allowing them to live in Palestine—a name the Romans gave to Israel. This dispersion or diaspora has lasted, historically, from that time until the establishment of the state of Israel in 1948.) Jesus spoke to his world—Matthew interprets for his world. Jesus' world was Galilee—Matthew's world was Antioch. Jesus' world was Israel (Jews)—Matthew's world was the Church (Jew and Gentile).

I wonder what this parable meant for Jesus' world. Perhaps verses 18-23 can answer that! We know clearly what it meant for Matthew's world. He tells us himself:

Seed on the path = those in Matthew's community who hear without understanding and are overtaken by the "evil one" (a cryptic name given to the Romans). This would be those Christian Gentiles in Matthew's community who, after converting to Christianity, returned to paganism.

Seed on rocky soil = those without roots who waver eventually. Christian Jews in Matthew's community who, under pressure from other Jews, gave up their Christianity.

Seed among briers = Gentile and Jewish Christians whose personal gain was more important than their commitment to the common good—the Christian community.

Seed on good soil = those Jews and Gentiles in Matthew's community who held on to their faith in Jesus in spite of persecution by Romans, pressure by Jews, and the temptations of the world.

What does this parable mean in *your* world?

24.
THE KINGDOM OF GOD IN MATTHEW'S GOSPEL

Reading: Matthew 13: 24-43

Upon reading these three parables of Jesus in Matthew's Gospel, I have two reflections, each of which ends with a question—a question, perhaps no one will be able to answer, nor do I intend that *you* should have an answer, but simply to reflect on the questions.

My first reflection is about the Kingdom of God. As you may have noticed, every description or image or parable about the Kingdom of God—even when interpreted by Jesus himself—is about *this world*. Although Jesus speaks about the end of the world, he still says: "The Son of (People) will send his angels, and they will collect out of his kingdom all who cause others to sin and all evildoers." Evildoers and those who draw others to sin are found in *this world*. If the Son of (People) collects these people from his kingdom, then he is collecting them from *this world*.

My first question is: Is *this world* the Kingdom of God? Or is the kingdom another world somewhere else? Jesus speaks of the end of the world. But do we not do the same? Do we not say things like "This is not the same world as when I was a child" or "The world my grandfather grew up in is different than the world in which I am now living"? The world, then, is both different and the same—like the ocean, different, but always the same—like people, different from one another, yet the same as each other. And so, let me leave you with my first question phrased slightly different, yet the same: Can this world become the Kingdom of God?

This is my second reflection: Did you notice that in each parable Jesus never literally says what the Kingdom of God is—only what it's *like?* "The reign of God may be *likened* to a man who sowed...The reign of God is *like* a mustard seed...The reign of God is *like* yeast..." Perhaps in making these metaphors and similes, Jesus is expressing his own hope about the kingdom rather than any knowledge he might have had!

My second question then is: Did Jesus know literally what the Kingdom of God is? All of his talking about the Kingdom was in parables, in images, metaphors, and similes. All we can discern from this is that deep within himself, Jesus had faith that there was a Kingdom of God, but as to what it was literally or where it was going to be or how it was to come about, there is no mention by him. And so the question again is: Did Jesus, literally, know what the Kingdom of God is?

Let us ponder and reflect on these two questions—questions that maybe Matthew never intended us to ask—questions neither he nor us can answer—but no less valid: Can this world become the Kingdom of God? Did Jesus literally know what the Kingdom of God is?

25.
WISDOM IN MATTHEW'S GOSPEL

Readings: I Kings 3:5-12 Romans 8:28-30 Matthew 13:44-52

Throughout the above readings, the terms WISDOM—UNDERSTANDING—KINGDOM OF GOD—REIGN OF GOD are all synonymous. All of these terms have the same meaning. We will discover that meaning as we go on!

In the First Book of Kings, we find a story about one of the greatest and wisest men who ever lived—King Solomon! In this story, Solomon is still a young king and has never exercised his authority. As king he is expected to have the capacity of distinguishing between good and evil. To make things more complex, the kingdom over which he has power is not his own, but rather God's. Solomon prays to God and his prayer reflects his great disquiet as he confronts his duties as king. In moments like this—prayer is the only recourse.

At first reading we might get the wrong idea about the prayer of Solomon. However, in Paul's Letter to the Romans, he tells us that prayer cannot be considered some sort of escape to God, but rather a joint recognition by God and people of their involvement with the universe. People and God will be partners, toiling and struggling together in a universe that is sometimes evil and recalcitrant. As we read in Matthew 13:30, good and evil will live together, until the time decided upon by God. Therefore, we should seek the Kingdom of God! Just as Solomon chose understanding above all else, the Christian is asked to choose the Kingdom of God in preference to worldly considerations.

So then, let me ask some poignant questions: Why do you continue to live? Why not commit suicide? Why don't you want to die—now—any way you like? I suspect your answer might be probably because of *curiosity*. You are curious! We want to know what else is there in life! What am I going to miss! Where is this life leading humankind! Where is it leading me! Will this someday be a "Planet of The Apes"? First water—then land—then air—then space—now the moon—what's next!? We are curious to know—what is this all about! What am I doing in this life! Every one of us wants to know all things. Every one of us seeks an understanding of what we see, hear, taste, smell or touch.

When did the First World War begin and why? What is the shortest distance between two points? Why does a cat have whiskers? How far is the planet Jupiter from the earth?—All of these questions have answers. Questions that have answers do not arouse our curiosity. These are not the things we seek to understand! Our search for understanding, like King Solomon's, is deeper. We are in search of understanding those things that have no answer, nor can be found in a book, which cannot be worked out on a blackboard nor in a laboratory.

It seemed a few years ago that churches stopped giving answers. Maybe the Church finally realized that by doing this she would lead her people to a deeper understanding of themselves, of life, and of God. The trite answers of the past did not satisfy our search for understanding, but only satisfied us for the moment, added to our body of knowledge, and kept us secure. The Gospel tells us: the search for understanding can be found only in seeking the Kingdom of God. Because as Jesus, himself, tells us in the Gospel, when you discover it you will run out and sell all that you own in order to gain it. A poet of our own times tells the story like this:

> *God was walking around the universe. All the solar systems and the nebulous stars ran under his feet like a field. Then he found a treasure, lying hidden in the field. It was this earth, with a man on it. And in his joy, he sold all that he had, his omnipotence and his all-seeing eye, his heaven and his hell, and bought the earth.**

And so, the Kingdom is here! This earth! People! Men and women! Children! And within each person there is hidden a treasure. And we must go searching for that treasure, that wisdom, that understanding, that kingdom. But *we* can only discover it if another person lets us, if they open themselves to us. And *they* can only discover it, if we open ourselves to them.

And as we go looking for that treasure in this person, in that person, or even in ourselves, we might discover life, perhaps eternal life, perhaps...God!

*At Times I See, Huub Oosterhuis, Seabury Press, 1974

26.
GENTILES IN THE GOSPEL OF MATTHEW

Readings: Isaiah 56:1,6-7 Romans 11:13-15,29-32 Matthew 15:21-28

My house shall be called a house of prayer for all peoples" (Isaiah). "Inasmuch as I am the apostle to the Gentiles, I glory in my ministry" (Paul to the Romans). "I was sent only to the lost sheep of the house of Israel" (Matthew).

The message of these three readings rings clear: All are welcome to share in Israel's privileges, for God's mercy is for all humankind. Jesus, himself, attests to the great faith of a foreigner, a Gentile—the Canaanite woman.

The destiny of the Gentile nations and the meaning of their religious pilgrimage was a constant worry to Israel. We experience this in all three writers (Isaiah, Paul, and Matthew). This worry could hardly have been otherwise, for Israel was never an isolated nation. She had numerous contacts not only with neighboring tribes, but with the great civilizations of the time: Egypt, Assyria, Babylon, and others. During the time of the Babylonian exile, Israel was dispersed and practically everywhere. In and among foreign peoples, there were Jewish communities.

Israel's associations with these other nations were always strained and determined by religion. She had to defend her right to existence as well as preserve her religious identity. She did not exclude the Gentiles entirely since there was a vision of the future when God's infinite mercy would reach out to all nations. God chose Israel, but was not uninterested in the other nations.

With the coming of Jesus, the Messiah, a different emphasis is given to the mission of Israel. God is concerned with *all* of humanity—*all* people are brothers and sisters dependent on God as Father. Jesus' ministry is revealing. He does not seek out the Gentiles. His mission is to Israel whom he prepares as witnesses among all the peoples of the earth. Jesus teaches that before God all people are brothers and sisters, that the Spirit works among the Gentiles as well and that their religious experience has meaning. "O woman, great is your faith" (Matt. 15:28). As time goes on, Israel refuses the thinking of the Messiah and this accents the universality of his message. The mission that was once reserved for Israel is now entrusted to any person who follows Jesus and agrees to obey his new commandment of love without limits. Jesus shows that religion and life are one! Insofar as a person devotes his or her life to others, whether that person realizes it or not, he or she is on the way to an encounter with Jesus.

The Second Vatican Council of the Roman Catholic Church was voicing this same conviction when it offered the dynamic concept of the Church that has no boundaries, no limits except those of humanity itself. And a dynamic concept of the people of God suggests a dynamic concept of the non-Christian as well. The non-Christian is a person journeying toward Christ, insofar as he or she is involved in the service of people. Even the atheist must be regarded as a brother or sister, who shares the human condition. The mission of the people of God is to encounter all people as they are and where they are, always bearing witness to the commandment of love. Since Vatican II we are becoming more fully aware that always seeking to convert people must definitely be replaced by dialogue. The Christian mission is a mission to dialogue!

But how can we do this? How can we dialogue without being an ordained minister or theologian? How can we dialogue about so many uncertain questions? How can we dialogue about religion?

If these questions bother us—then maybe we are the ones in need of conversion—and not the non-Christians!

And there is no better place for this conversion to take place than among our brothers and sisters inside our churches. For all our assemblies should be assemblies for all people, and this is particularly true when we assemble on Sundays for the breaking of the bread. Every Eucharistic celebration should reach out to all humanity and exhibit what it means to be truly Christian. When Christ gives us his body and blood, he is giving us all people as brothers and sisters in faith...for we are his body—every man, woman and child—every human being who has gone before us, is, and is to come.

If we really believe this—then we are the true Israel, the Church, a people fit to dialogue with each other in the Spirit for the service of all humankind.

27.
STORIES OF POWER IN MATTHEW'S GOSPEL

Readings: Isaiah 22:15, 19-23 Romans 11:33-36 Matthew 16:13-20

The prophet Isaiah presents us with a picture of a happening that connects us to the account that we read in the Gospel. It is the detailed description of the investiture of a certain royal functionary by the name of Eliakim. His robe, sash, and above all the keys are the insignia of his office. The keys symbolize the extent of his power and the opening and closing of the door foreshadow the "locking and unlocking," which are also spoken of in the Gospel. A person who is entrusted with the keys is the one who has the power!

Paul's letter to the Romans reminds the believer that all that exists comes from God. The power that any person has or will pass on to others comes from God. The old saying, "All authority comes from God," is the message of Paul to us, and he insists that we therefore give glory to God.

In the Gospel of Matthew we have the story of Jesus passing on his power to Peter. The early Christian community (who obviously tampered with Matthew's Gospel) places this passage above as if it was before the resurrection and yet the mission given to Peter is a post-resurrection one.

However, let us take a look at some of the previous passages and see what significance they play in the account we read from above:

• The multiplication of the loaves and fishes indicated and pointed to CHRIST'S POWER OVER BREAD (Matt.14:13-21)

• Jesus walking on the water indicated and pointed to CHRIST'S POWER OVER HIS BODY (Matt. 14:22-27)

• Jesus calming the sea and wind indicated and pointed to CHRIST'S POWER OVER THE ELEMENTS (Matt. 14:28-33)

• Jesus curing the Canaanite woman's daughter of a demon indicated and pointed to CHRIST'S POWER OVER EVIL (Matt. 15:21-28)

• Peter making his profession of faith in Jesus indicated and pointed to CHRIST'S POWER OVER PEOPLE (Matt. 16:13-20)

In all of these accounts, Matthew points to various incidents in the life of Jesus that prove his power. And in the passage above, Jesus gives his power to the whole Church in the person of Peter. He does this through the sign value of keys! "I will give you the keys to the kingdom of heaven" (Matt. 16:19). Keys are the sign of power, because in actual life, as in the story from Isaiah, the one who has keys has the power to open or close...to give or not give...to permit or not permit...to stop or start...to say yes or no! For example, if you gave someone the keys to your house, wouldn't you say that they have the same power as you do over all you possess?

In Matthew's Gospel, no longer was this power reserved to Israel alone—this power would be extended to Gentiles as well, through the Church.

And so, the power of Christ was given to the Church and with all authority that is Christ's to give. "Whatever you bind on earth, will be bound in heaven; whatever you loose on earth shall be loosed in heaven" (Matt. 16:19).

This power is not just to forgive sins, but includes all things that the Church will set about to accomplish in Christ's name. Therefore the Church is filled with this power:

The power of prayer...

The power of healing...

The power of love...

The power of faith...

The power of forgiveness...

The power of hope...

The power over death...

The power over bread and wine...

The power over evil...

The power to create...

The power to free...

The power to live life to the fullest!

All this has been given to *us*—for we are the Church! The Church becomes the foundation, the rock, upon which the Kingdom of God is to be built. We are the Body of Christ with all the power that is his! The question is: What are we going to do with all this power? What *are* we doing with all this power? How can we cause this power to become effective in the world?

I think we really do **not** believe this! If we **really** believed—**really believed**—that we **are** the Body of Christ, and that we have this power, then we would **use** this power to transform the world into the Kingdom of God!

28.
THE FIRST OF THE VINEYARD PARABLES IN
MATTHEW

Readings: Isaiah 55:6-9 Matthew 20:1-16

The parable we just read can be found *only* in the Gospel of Matthew. It seems to belong to the early *Jewish* Christians. The example used by Jesus is one connected to the Hellenistic-Roman lifestyle of our early Church.

The parable compares the Jews and the Gentiles in the Reign of God. The workmen hired at dawn and midmorning would be the Jews of the Old Testament. The workmen hired at noon and midafternoon would be the Jews of the New Testament. The workmen hired last in the late afternoon would be the Gentiles. The owner of the vineyard is God and the vineyard is the kingdom.

The Gentiles were admitted into Christianity later, but they were admitted on equal standing with the Jews. We all know from Paul's letters and the Acts of the Apostles that the controversy over the admission of the Gentiles into the early Church was a major problem and that it was ultimately solved in the manner indicated in the parable we just read. This parable indicates that an early call into the Christian community has no relevance to status in the Reign of God. Whenever one is admitted into the Reign of God, one is admitted to full participation. The Reign of God is not the property of those who first sought admission.

When you and I look at this parable, we usually react the same way as the workmen who were hired earliest. We demand justice, fairness, our due! We tend to claim that the first should be first and the last should be last. We expect this, especially from God. But that is our way, our thoughts. From the prophet Isaiah we hear, "For my thoughts are not your thoughts, nor are your ways my ways, says the Lord" (Is. 55:8). Isaiah continues by saying that our God is merciful and generous. And there's the problem—*we* demand justice, and *God* is generous! Which is of the greater value, justice or generosity?

In this parable, Jesus teaches that being graceful and generous is far greater than justice and fairness. We live in a world where the cry for justice and fairness are misused for one's own good to the detriment of our fellow human beings. We live in a world where "equality" is a concept found in archaic documents such as the Bible or the US Constitution, only to be quoted and not to be lived. In our world, the first are first and the last are last! In our world, the first get more and the last get less! In our world, there are kings and super gods, the powerful and the powerless, queens and slaves, masters and servants!

The world, envisioned in the Gospel, is an upside-down world where the last shall be first and the first shall be last. It is a world where no one is king; no one is god; no one! It is a world where all people are equal and grace abounds, even over distributive justice and generosity.

This was Matthew's vision for his Church—for all Christians!

If Matthew was calling upon *all* his fellow Christians to live this way, imagine how much more of a responsibility it is to be a leader or minister responding to this call. Leadership and ministry in a community of equals is an awesome responsibility. It means not acting as a god or king, but as a servant. It means not only being fair, but being generous. It means loving those we lead and leading those we love. It means remaining equal while doing an unequalled task. It means being "graceful." It means seeing as God sees—expressed so well in that wisdom riddle, "The last shall be first and the first shall be last."

What that means is—in God's eyes, we are all equal! Why are we not equal in each other's eyes?!

29.
THE SECOND VINEYARD PARABLE IN MATTHEW

Readings: Ezekiel 18:25-28 Philippians 2:1-11 Matthew 21:28-32

This second vineyard parable is no different from the first in that we can deduce exactly *who* Matthew is talking about with each character. All three of the vineyard parables deal with Matthew's obsession with the fact that some of his own people—the Jews—have refused to accept Jesus as the Messiah. Let us look closely at this parable to determine a message.

Notice first that Jesus is addressing the chief priests and elders of the people. These men stood (or were supposed to stand) for everything that Israel believed in. It is fitting then that Matthew has Jesus confronting these particular men with this parable. The elder son in the parable represents Israel who promises to work in the vineyard, yet does not. The younger son in the parable represents the wayward, or so-called "lost sheep" of Israel, who never made any promises, but in the end had a conversion and did work in the vineyard. The vineyard is once again the Kingdom of God. The man with the two sons is God.

Matthew makes the parable clear when Jesus says: "Let me make it clear that tax collectors and prostitutes are entering the Kingdom of God before you" (Matt. 21:31). Now remember, Jesus is addressing the chief priests and elders. It would be as if he were addressing your pastor or governor, or mayor. So, you see the impact this parable had on the people who were present. These men were looked up to and respected. They were the examples, the leaders. They were the ones who stood for all that was "Israel." And yet, Jesus condemns them—but most especially Matthew condemns them for not accepting Jesus as Messiah.

Almost as though he were making a commentary on this parable, the Prophet Ezekiel says: "When someone virtuous turns away from virtue to commit iniquity, and dies, it is because of the iniquity he committed that he must die. But if he turns from the wickedness he has committed, and does what is right and just, he shall preserve his life; since he has turned away from all the sins that he has committed, he shall surely live, he shall not die" (Ez. 18:26-28).

The message of this parable is similar to the first: Everyone has an equal chance to enter the Kingdom of God! It makes no difference what mistakes we make in life—these can always be forgiven. We shouldn't look down on ourselves—and perhaps we shouldn't always look so naively at those who hold some status in the church or government, or those who find it so easy to judge everyone else's faults. It will be just as hard for the virtuous person to enter the Kingdom as it will be for the wicked. God plays favorites with no one—not even his own Son—as the next "vineyard" parable will explain.

So, remember again—"The last shall be first, and the first shall be last" (Matt. 20:16). What that means is—that in God's eyes we are all equal! My question again is—why aren't we equal in each other's eyes?

30.
THE THIRD VINEYARD PARABLE IN MATTHEW

Readings: Isaiah 5:1-7 Matthew 21:33-43

If we looked for this parable from the Gospel of Matthew in other Scripture passages, we would find it in Mark's and Luke's Gospels and the apocryphal Gospel of Thomas. In Luke and Thomas, the story told by Jesus is just that—a story—to be taken literally—with a lesson to be drawn from it: "See," Jesus says, "how these vinedressers stopped at nothing. They even murdered the heir to get hold of the vineyard. You must be just as resolute in laying hold of the kingdom of God!" In other words—if we take this parable and draw a lesson from it—the lesson would be that each of us has been presented with the challenge to *seize hold* of the Gospel—to be aggressive in our desire to live the message of Jesus...to live the Gospel! In Mark, this parable is a call to individual repentance!

Now, let's go back to the rendition of this parable from Matthew. We see that he has intentions of echoing the passages from Isaiah and giving (instead of a story with a lesson) a story with allegory—that is, a story with a hidden meaning that needs interpretation. Here is the early Church's interpretation:

The vineyard symbolizes Israel...

The owner symbolizes God the Father...

The first group of slaves symbolizes the Old Testament prophets...

The second group of slaves symbolizes the apostles of the New Testament...The owner's son symbolizes Jesus himself...

The tenants are the scribes and the elders...

The killing of the owner's son symbolizes the crucifixion...

Jesus' suggestion that the Kingdom of God be taken away symbolizes the Church leaving Judaism and becoming Gentile...

Notice also the use of vineyard (a place where grapes are grown to make wine). Later in Matthew's Gospel, Jesus calls the wine his "blood, poured out for the forgiveness of sin" (Matt. 26:28).

Here you have three explanations: 1) The first is a call to individual repentance. 2) The second is a lesson asking us to live the Gospel message. 3) The third is an allegory symbolizing a summation of the Plan of Salvation. These three are one and the same thing! For through the Gospel we discover a God who has created life and asks us to live it to the fullest (by *seizing* the Gospel). Then, through the coming and life of Jesus, we have revealed that God's plan of life is one of redemption, salvation, freedom, and liberation from anything that would destroy the life God has created.

Life is so sacred that God gave it to us as God's greatest gift—God gave Godself to us in creation and in the person of God's Son—again, God gave Godself for us!

If we see and believe this, why do we still want to seize life and kill it, destroy it, suffocate it? Why do people find it so necessary to kill unborn children and have abortions? Why are people so selfish that poverty runs rampant alongside of abundance and waste? Why do we destroy our bodies by overeating, smoking, taking drugs, and abusing alcohol? Why do we destroy the plants and animals for fun or sport? Why are people prejudiced and small-minded enough to curtail the fullness of life for people who are of a different color, belief, or even sex than they? Why do we suffocate the elderly by ignoring them or putting them away somewhere? Why is there such a thing as a "death penalty?" Why are crime and violence in our country and elsewhere on the upsurge? Why do we always have war somewhere in our world?

You might find yourself asking these same questions! You probably understand all too well, especially when it occurs in your own life. I'm sure you don't deny the need for people to live as Jesus lived—giving life, restoring life, living for others. Then I must ask you—you who profess to live as he lived—What are *you* doing to respect the life we have been given!? What are *you* doing to make it a better life for everyone?

31.
MORE ABOUT THE KINGDOM IN MATTHEW'S GOSPEL

Readings: Isaiah 25:6-10a Matthew 22:1-14

In Matthew's Gospel the kingdom has been likened to a mustard seed, which is small at first, but then blooms into something great. The kingdom has been likened to a farmer who sows the seed on all sorts of ground (rocky, thorny, and good soil) to find only the good soil worthy and producing a rich harvest. The kingdom has been likened to a vineyard where one may enter to work at any hour and receive the same wages. The kingdom has been likened to a vineyard where the tenants lose their rights because they are greedy. The kingdom is described as one in which prostitutes, tax collectors, and publicans will enter before even the priests and leaders of the people.

In the passage above, Matthew likens the kingdom to a wedding banquet given by a king for his son. This parable is very similar to the rest. The same message is delivered, but a new and important dimension is discovered if we look closely. By now you are able to discern that the king is God and his son is Jesus. The first group of servants who go to summon the invited guests are the prophets of the Old Testament. The invited guests are the people of Israel from Abraham to Jesus. These guests refuse to come to the banquet. The second group of servants who go to summon the invited guests are the apostles of the New Testament. The invited guests who again refuse are the people of Israel who have already rejected Jesus, crucified him, and then proceeded to do the same to the apostles, insulting and killing them. The king is then furious, destroys the murderers, burns their city (probably a reference to the fall of Jerusalem to the Romans in 70 CE) and dispatches a third group of servants to invite anyone to the banquet. This reference, as in all the other parables of Matthew, indicates the invitation to the Gentiles, the non-Jews, into the kingdom. The third group of servants who do this are the early Christian Church, those Jews who accepted Jesus.

Here, therefore, is the unique characteristic found in this parable. The Kingdom of God would be filled by anyone (Jew or Gentile), bad as well as good, as long as they accepted the invitation and were willing to commit themselves fully to living in God's Kingdom. No halfhearted or curious people would be able to live in this kingdom—only those who fully accepted the invitation and wished to give even their lives to live up to this commitment. Being born a Jew was no longer the only status in God's Kingdom. One had to be more than just born into a certain environment; one had to be totally willing to accept the invitation, and through God's Son, even the Gentiles could do this—all people—bad as well as good. Thus, that poor guy who comes to the banquet without a wedding garment—hesitant, halfhearted, curious, relying on his status as a Jew, finds himself turned away.

Sometimes there are some of us like the man without a wedding garment. We cling to our status in the Church! We come to the banquet halfheartedly, not really sure we want to be there, not dressed for the occasion, but content that someone once had us baptized as children, cajoled us into making our first communion, and forced us to be confirmed. Some of us would rather be somewhere else—we're bored, looking at our watch, basically halfhearted, using any excuse not to return. Some of us come to the banquet out of fear—fear that our status in the Church demands this of us or we will be punished for eternity if we do not—and so we come not dressed for the occasion. We have no wedding garment. Sometimes we are even bold enough to criticize those who are not of our status, not of our color, not of our belief, not of our nation—and at the same time, we remain uncommitted, doing the minimum, keeping the law, refusing to wear a wedding garment.

"The invited are many—the elect are few!" The Kingdom of God will be given only to those who come fully committed to the work of the kingdom (fully dressed in a wedding garment). No race alone can claim this kingdom, no one nationality alone can own it, no one religion alone can possess it. For the Christian, the kingdom is founded on Jesus and is for anyone and everyone who is committed to taking the risk—the risk to live life as Jesus lived it. To live as he lived is to love our neighbor, to have a certain sensitivity toward others, with the absence of contempt and mistrust, and the presence of openness, and a desire to understand and share. There is room for everyone in his kingdom—there is food for everyone at his banquet—no one will be hungry for you can eat as much as you like...

But before you enter—please put on a wedding garment!

32.
A STORY IN MATTHEW'S GOSPEL

Readings: Isaiah 45:1, 4-6 Matthew 22:15-22

This story we just read from the Gospel of Matthew can also be found in the gospels of Mark and Luke, as well. It is not found in any form in the fourth Gospel—the Gospel of John.

Scholars today believe that Matthew and Luke used Mark's Gospel as the basis for their own gospels and at times copied Mark word for word, and at other times adjusted (redacted) Mark's Gospel radically. Interestingly enough, the story we read above appears in all three gospels with few variances. I believe there is a lesson in the closing verse of each of these gospels' rendition of this story. The original writer—Mark—concludes with this line: "Their amazement at him knew no bounds" (Mark 12:17b). Matthew's Gospel says: "Taken aback by this reply, they went off and left him" (Matt. 22:22). The closing line in Luke's Gospel reads: "They were unable to trap him publicly in speech. His answer completely disconcerted them and reduced them to silence" (Luke 20:26).

I suggest, therefore, that all three synoptic writers—Mark, Matthew and Luke—are saying that Jesus did **not** answer the question that was posed to him. Instead, he offered a vital instruction to his Jewish audience.

In the law of Israel, the first commandment that God uttered on Sinai is to have no images of God. Statues, pictures, sculptures, coins, etc. describing or imaging God were forbidden. The reason is that Israel believed and envisioned a God of mystery—unfathomable and indefinable. For Israel, the definition of God was the One who has no definition, is pure spirit and cannot be imaged in art.

In contrast to this is the earthly ruler (in this case the Emperor of Rome) whose statue and bust were everywhere—and whose image was even on the money (similar to our money today with Washington on the dollar bill, etc.).

Jesus sets the scene for his lesson and punch line by asking for a coin...(notice—he didn't have one of his own). The God of Israel is obeyed *without* being seen or depicted or hanging constantly in view of the obedient. God is found in the Law, the Torah. The earthly ruler is not equal to God since he has to threaten his subjects into submission with his image and face on every street corner and even on the coins they carry in their pockets.

What a contrast! God and Caesar! The Invisible and the visible! Divine and human! For Israel—God is the King! For Israel—the king and God are one and the same! For Israel—God is her one and only king! For Israel—only God can anoint a human to accomplish the divine plan and lead people into this plan, as was Cyrus, the King of Persia, mentioned in the reading from Isaiah. In Israel—no human is God and no human is king!

And now—the punch line: "Then repay to Caesar what belongs to Caesar and to God what belongs to God" (Matt. 22:21).

33.
THE PARABLE OF THE WISE AND FOOLISH IN MATTHEW'S GOSPEL

Readings: Wisdom 6:12-16 Psalm 139 Matthew 25:1-13

The key to understanding the Scripture above is in the biblical concept of "wisdom." In the Book of Wisdom, wisdom is praised as unfading—unwavering—dependable—faithful! Psalm 139 speaks of wisdom as God's thoughts and that the world is full of this wisdom. Finally in the Gospel, the virgins with wisdom are those who are prepared and ready for the bridegroom's return.

Note the components or symbols in the Gospel parable: ten bridesmaids (five foolish and five wise ones), the bridegroom, oil, the wedding banquet. Now, remember who wrote this Gospel—Matthew. Recall the status of this Jewish-Christian community who produced this Gospel. And now let's interpret the parable: The ten bridesmaids are those Jews who accepted Christianity and are now members of Matthew's community living in Antioch around the year 80 CE. Remember—the image of Israel in the Old Testament is often a "bride." In the Old Testament, God is often referred to as the "bridegroom." Thus in this parable, the bridegroom is Jesus, whose return is expected at any moment. The wedding banquet is, of course, the Kingdom of God into which Jesus will lead those who are faithful and awake, and await his coming with vigilance.

The five *foolish* virgins symbolize those members of Matthew's community who were losing faith, doubting, wavering, nodding off to sleep, and losing patience and endurance. The five *wise* virgins symbolize those members of Matthew's community who were steadfast in faith, unwavering, unfading, dependable, always awake, patient, and expectant. The *oil* is the ingredient that determines faith*ful*ness from faith*less*ness; that determines endurance from submission; that determines patience from impatience; that determines strength from weakness; that determines wisdom from folly.

For Matthew, as for the writer of the Book of Wisdom, the *wise* are those with enough oil to last as long as it takes in a time of crisis or period of darkness. The *foolish* are those who do not have enough oil to last through a crisis or delay or long period of endurance.

It is obvious from the presence of this parable in the Gospel, that Matthew's community contained some Jewish Christians who were beginning to waver in their faith about Jesus. These "foolish" members had lost all endurance and strength (in other words, their "oil") and their lamps or torches (their faith) were slowly dying out.

So, Matthew appeals to their sense of history in this parable, their knowledge of the Hebrew Scripture, their awareness that in the Old Testament wisdom is always aligned with hope and folly with despair. And so, he tells of the *wise* and *foolish* bridesmaids, to bring home to his audience, that those who lose heart and falter will not make it into God's Kingdom. Only the wise will be admitted. For wisdom **is** endurance, faithfulness, and dependability. And that these are God's thoughts and God's ways. God had always remained faithful to Israel despite her foolish ways. It certainly can't be that hard for her now to remain faithful to God for just a short time longer.

That's what the parable means to Matthew's audience. Where are **you** in this parable?

34.
THE GOSPEL OF LUKE

Reading: Luke 1:1-4

What do we learn from these short verses? That Luke is not an eyewitness. And he is giving his reason for writing a Gospel. He is writing an orderly account for the Gentile, Theophilus.

Luke probably wrote his Gospel in approximately 80 CE. His sources are Mark and Matthew and oral tradition. Luke handles the material taken from these sources respectfully, but never slavishly. He insinuates his own viewpoint with delicate tact. For the sake of a smooth literary style, he makes many omissions—details that would bore his Gentile readers and incidents that would disrupt his overall plan. Luke also retouches and expands his material. So, although we find many elements that are similar to those in Mark and Matthew, we also find stories that appear in no other Gospel. For example, the story of the shepherds at the birth of Jesus is exclusively Luke's, as is the story of the disciples on the road to Emmaus. Many parables such as the Prodigal Son, the Good Samaritan, the Rich Fool and the Shrewd Manager appear only in Luke's Gospel.

It is interesting to see how Luke uses these stories as teaching devices. For instance, in Mark's Gospel, a lawyer comes to Jesus with the question, "Teacher, what must I do to inherit eternal life?" Jesus asks him a question in return, to which he answers, "Love your neighbor as yourself." Only in Luke does the lawyer persist with another question, "And who is my neighbor?" At this point Luke relates the parable of the Good Samaritan (Luke 10:25-37). It is as if Luke wants to make it completely clear who one's neighbor is, and how he should be loved. It is also interesting to note how Luke expands and changes events that are simply mentioned in Mark's Gospel. For example, while Mark mentions that Jesus was crucified between two thieves who reviled him, Luke takes this information and builds around it the story of the Good Thief.

Luke writes primarily for Gentiles somewhere in Greece and for their sake makes many changes in the Gospel tradition. I suspect that this is one of the reasons why Luke is so easy for us to read today. Although we realize that we as Christians come from Jewish origins, we have pathetically little knowledge of Jewish customs and Jewish Scripture. Luke, writing for Gentiles, understands this problem and deals with it in several ways: 1) The first is to simply omit the problem words. For instance, in Matthew's and Mark's crucifixion accounts, Jesus cries out in a loud voice, "Eli, Eli, (Eloi Eloi) lema sabachthani?" Luke drops this whole episode from his account; 2) Another way that Luke deals with this problem of language is to translate the word, rather than use the word and then translate it. For example, in Mark we read, "And they brought him to the place called Golgotha (which means the place of the skull)." In Luke it is simply, "They came to the place which is called The Skull"; and 3) Finally, Luke will find substitutes for words when necessary. So, Luke alone uses the word "alive" to describe the risen Christ. Aware that Gentile readers might have problems with the term resurrection, Luke substitutes the term "life," which has meaning for both the Greek and the Jewish worlds.

As we can see from these examples, Luke is an original writer as well as an Evangelist. In his attempt to give an orderly account, he needs really, to write two Gospels. The first is a description of the events regarding Jesus' earthly life. The first Gospel begs for a sequel. When we finish reading the Gospel of Luke we are itching, indeed, encouraged to ask, "What happened next?" And Luke answers by picking up where he left off in a second volume called Acts of the Apostles.

In writing the two volumes, Luke presents the events in an orderly temporal framework: Jesus' earthly life, his death, his resurrection, appearances that occur for forty days (mentioned only in the Acts of the Apostles), his ascension into heaven (which is described in both the Gospel and the Acts) and the descent of the spirit at Pentecost (which is mentioned only in the Acts of the Apostles). No other Gospel writer uses this particular time line.

In summary, here are some points about Luke and his Gospel:

1. He wants to write an orderly account.
2. Written around 80 CE.
3. Written for Gentiles (Greece).

4. Uses Mark's and perhaps Matthew's Gospel as a major source.

5. Original material (stories not found in any other Gospel), as teaching devices.

6. Changes material from Mark and Matthew to fit his audience and to teach (omits, changes, or translates and substitutes words).

7. Specific time line: Annunciation—birth—twelve years old—genealogy—ministry at thrirty years old—adult life—death—resurrection—forty days of appearances—ascension—fifty days Pentecost).

8. Two volumes (Gospel and Acts of Apostles).

Who was Luke?

1. A Gentile Christian. Some scholars speculate that Luke was originally Gentile, then converted to Judaism and then to Christianity.

2. A storyteller.

3. A teacher.

4. An Evangelist.

5. An original writer.

6. A stickler for details and time lines.

35.
THEMES IN THE GOSPEL OF LUKE

L uke uses seven major themes that run throughout his Gospel and the Acts of the Apostles and gives them a literary unity. In this sermon, I will deal with five of them. The sixth and seventh major themes I will deal with in sermons to follow.

1) The first and most obvious theme is Luke's use of the city of Jerusalem. Throughout the Gospel, Jerusalem is the focal point, the turning point in a life. Thus, events in or a journey to Jerusalem is always significant. In fact, Luke begins his Gospel in the temple in Jerusalem. There it is revealed to Zechariah that his wife, Elizabeth, would bear a son, John the Baptist. To Jerusalem also Mary and Joseph take the baby Jesus to be presented in the temple. There Simeon and the prophetess, Anna, recognize Jesus as the salvation of Israel. Again, when Jesus is twelve, he is taken to Jerusalem for the feast of Passover. Jesus remains behind in the city and amazes the teachers of the temple with his understanding and knowledge. In Luke's Gospel, Jesus begins his adult ministry in Galilee and it is there, in Galilee, that Jesus remains until the time is right for him to go to Jerusalem, where the saving events will occur. After the death of Jesus, it is in Jerusalem (not Galilee as it is in Mark and Matthew) that Jesus appears to the assembled disciples. And it is in Jerusalem that the disciples await the coming of the Spirit. It is at this point that Luke ends his Gospel and begins the Acts of the Apostles—waiting for the Spirit in Jerusalem.

2) The second major theme in Luke is the mystery of the divine plan. Luke is a theologian of history, or, to use the language of faith, a theologian of God's plan. Throughout his Gospel, Luke is never content to merely describe an event. He must explain it, interpret it, within the great plan of God as revealed through Scripture. Thus, the scandal of Jesus' death on the cross is removed by placing it within the great plan of God.

3) The third major theme in Luke's Gospel is that it is known as the Gospel of reconciliation. The Jew/Gentile issue that rocked the early

church is solved by Luke: he makes Mary and Elizabeth cousins. Mary represents the New Testament Gentile Church and Elizabeth represents the Old Testament Judaism; Luke suggests that the issue is simply a family feud and can be solved if we recognize that Jews and Gentiles are not enemies. Luke goes so far in his many attempts at reconciliation in his Gospel to reconcile even Herod with Pontius Pilate during Jesus' trial and the thief on the cross during Jesus' crucifixion. The angel Gabriel's line to Mary is the basis for this theme: "Nothing will be impossible for God" (Luke 1:37).

4) The fourth major theme is that this Gospel is known as the universal Gospel. Luke wrote to show that Jesus came for the salvation of all people—not just to Israel—but to the Gentiles as well. This is seen most clearly when Luke traces Jesus' genealogy back to Adam who is the father of the entire human race. In the Acts of the Apostles, Luke shows how the Church spreads from Jerusalem to the ends of the earth (symbolized by the city of Rome at the conclusion of the Acts).

5) The fifth theme is that Luke's Gospel is the Gospel of the poor and rejected—the good news for the lonely and outcasts. His message is that Jesus came to all people, and he rejected no one. For this very reason, he himself was rejected and crucified. Examples of these poor can be found in stories and characters found only in Luke's Gospel: Elizabeth (barren), Zachary (worn-out old priest), Mary and Joseph (the questionable unmarried ones), Anna and Simeon (the aged), shepherds (outcasts), the man with dropsy, the good Samaritan, the prodigal son, the shrewd manager, the poor man Lazarus, the ten lepers, the publican, the good thief, Zacchaeus (that little guy), the widow of Nain, the pagan centurion, the sinner woman with the oil, the ministering women (Mary Magdalene, Joanna, Susanna), the apostles (fishermen). These are known as the *Anawim*, that is, the poor remnant of Israel.

Once again, therefore, the seven major themes used by Luke are:

1) The city of Jerusalem (the birthplace of Christianity).

2) The mystery of God's plan (Christianity is God's plan).

3) The Gospel of reconciliation (Jesus brings all things and all people together).

4) Universal message (the destiny of Christianity to the Gentiles).

5) The Anawim (Christianity gives meaning to the poor and rejected).

6) The theme of women.
7) The theme of prayer and the Holy Spirit.

36.
THE THEME OF WOMEN IN LUKE'S GOSPEL

Reading: Luke 1:26-38

Thirty-five or forty years ago when many of us began to teach new ideas about the Bible, I would have never guessed, nor would the world in which we lived allow us to think, that the Gospel of Luke contained a very prominent theme of "women"; that the Gospel itself contained many feminine images; and that the hero of this Gospel was no hero at all, but a heroine, whose name is Mary.

The use of women in Luke's Gospel is dominant over other Gospels since he references "women" ten times in general, twice with regard to Mary, and in two different parables—a total of fourteen references to the specific theme of "women." In the Gospel also are six extraordinary references to a woman's "womb" and nine more references to the theme of "women" in his second volume, the Acts of the Apostles. It is also a Gospel where women—and not men—are the main actors (e.g., Elizabeth, Mary, and Anna).

I think Luke is being obvious, yet it has been only in recent times that we have come awake to his poignant theme of women.

May I state here what must be taken into consideration in any sermon of this nature—that I make a distinction between what is feminine and a woman, and what is masculine and a man. I recognize, along with you, that there is both feminine and masculine in every man and feminine and masculine in every woman. Otherwise, what I might say could seem sexist!

In the reading above, taken from chapter one of Luke's Gospel, we read the story of the annunciation of the birth of Jesus. If we agree with the Lucan theme of women and his use of the feminine throughout the Gospel, we can see that he is exposing this theme very early in his infancy narrative (chapters one and two), which can be looked upon as an introduction or prologue to his entire Gospel.

In the story of the annunciation, Luke uses the feminine image of a receptacle or vessel and applies it to a woman named Mary. God comes to a woman. God enters our world and finds a worthy receptacle in this woman, Mary. She neither fights nor doubts this activity of God. Instead, with her famous words, "I am the handmaid of the Lord. May it be done to me according to your word," she clearly opens herself to the presence and activity of God so as to become a worthy receptacle and vessel of God's revelation to our world.

We are left with this story of the annunciation, because Mary was open and accepting—a true vessel, a real receptacle for God's word and activity. She wasn't rigid and closed, insisting that if this was the God of Israel, "HE" should be active in Jerusalem, in the temple, in some priest. No, she was open to God who saw fit to enter the heart of a woman, in her home, in Nazareth.

So, this is not a story about women being feminine, or about women having babies, or about the dominance of a masculine God over a frail female mortal.

It is a story that points to the feminine in all of us—and what a blessing this femininity can be not only for us personally, but for the whole world, when we recognize that we must always be open and receptive to how, when, and where God will act in our lives.

In the Gospel of Luke, Mary becomes the heroine, because she recognizes this and cooperates with God in bringing about salvation.

Lest we men feel left out, it is in the Gospel of Matthew where a man, Joseph, recognizes *his* femininity, cooperates with God's activity, and also becomes an instrument of salvation for the world.

Often today, we hear authors and scholars talking about the femininity in Jesus—well, where did he get it from? He got it, of course, from Mary and Joseph, his mother and legal father.

To go one final step further—we also call Jesus the Son of God. Jesus received from God, his parent also, both the feminine and masculine of his being—no different than all of us who were "created in the image and likeness of God...in the divine image...male and female" (Gen. 1:27).

37.
THE PERSON, IMAGE, AND ROLE OF MARY IN LUKE'S GOSPEL

In every Gospel, there are themes, images or symbols, and characteristics that distinguish one Gospel from another. Under the umbrella of Luke's theme of the feminine and women in his Gospel, come the person, image, and role of Mary, the mother of Jesus.

In his book, *The Birth of the Messiah*, Father Raymond Brown has this to say about the role of Mary in Luke's Gospel:

"Luke is...interested in establishing the continuity of the Christian movement with Israel...His heroine, Mary, will embody that continuity—she responds obediently to God's word from the first as a representative of the Anawim of Israel (1:38); she appears in the ministry as a representative of the ideals of true discipleship (8:19-21); and she endures till Pentecost to become a Christian and a member of the Church (Acts 1:14)" (p. 499).

Let's examine the Gospel to see how Luke does this. On two major occasions in the ministry of Jesus, Luke interrupts his story of Jesus to insert these commentaries. In chapter eight, Jesus is telling parable after parable about the need to hear the word of God and respond to it. Then all of a sudden, this passage is inserted: "Then his mother and his brothers came to him but were unable to join him because of the crowd. He was told, 'Your mother and your brothers are standing outside and they wish to see you.' He said to them in reply, 'My mother and my brothers are those who hear the word of God and act on it'" (Luke 8:19-21). Later in chapter eleven, Jesus is again teaching the need to be open to God's word and this little passage is thrown in: "While he was speaking, a woman from the crowd called out and said to him, 'Blessed is the womb that carried you and the breasts at which you nursed.' He replies, 'Rather, blessed are those who hear the word of God and observe it'" (Luke 11:27-28).

As a child, both those passages used to upset me, since I thought Jesus was being disrespectful toward his mother. On the other hand, as I grew older and became more familiar with Luke's Gospel, I have learned that these passages are anything but disrespectful. They are affirmative praises of Mary who is the fulfillment of these verses.

Long before you reach these passages in Luke's Gospel, one hears these passages in chapter one. After hearing God's word from the angel Gabriel, Mary said: "I am the handmaid of the Lord. May it be done to me according to your word" (Luke 1:38). In other words—Mary hears God's word from the angel and welcomes it into her life. This is affirmed in a few verses later when she visits Elizabeth and Elizabeth says to her, "Most blessed are you among women" (Luke 1:42). "Blessed are you who believed that what was spoken to you by the Lord would be fulfilled" (Luke 1:45).

It is clear then, without any more proof that Luke intends to use Mary symbolically as the *disciple par excellence*—the one who hears the word of God and keeps it! Mary does three important things in Luke's mind—she was **open** to God's word…she **heard** God's word…she **lived** according to that word.

Mary stands out in the Gospel of Luke as the "mother" who becomes a "woman" and a "woman" who becomes a "disciple." Mary responds to God's word no matter what it asks of her. She is converted by God's word. Mary is the "mother" in whom God's word is carried to fulfillment. Mary is the "woman" in whom God's word found a hearing. Mary is the "disciple" in whom God's word is accomplished.

For Luke, there is something in the feminine that captures true discipleship. For Luke, discipleship is in the ability *to listen to, to hear, to internalize* the word of God, make sense of it, and then bring it to birth in one's actions and life. These are the female qualities in both men and women.

In this Gospel, women become the receptacles who are open and receptive to God's word, such as Elizabeth or the sinner who washed Jesus' feet with her hair. In this Gospel, even men exhibit this feminine quality of receptivity and openness—look at the shepherds who go immediately to Bethlehem, without questions, or the Prophet Simeon who immediately takes the baby Jesus into his arms and blesses him, or the good thief who is completely open to Jesus' invitation to paradise.

The message for us who are *listening* to this Gospel is that we will really *hear* it, so that God's word may be *conceived* in us as it was in Mary; that each of us—man or woman—may be willing to access the feminine side of ourselves, and like Mary, carry the word within our hearts; and then after an appropriate period of pregnancy allow ourselves to be reborn as true disciples of Jesus Christ.

38.
THE THEME OF PRAYER AND THE HOLY SPIRIT
IN LUKE

"I sing with all my soul and praise my God. My heart is glad because of God my savior." So prayed Mary, who conceived by the *Holy Spirit* (Luke 1:46-47).

Zechariah, filled with the *Holy Spirit,* uttered these words: "Blest are you, the God of salvation. You have come to set Israel free" (Luke 1:68).

Elizabeth, his wife, was also filled with the *Holy Spirit* and cried out in a loud voice: "Blest is she who trusted that God's words to her would be fulfilled" (Luke 1:45).

Simeon, who had the *Holy Spirit* upon him, had a revelation from the *Holy Spirit,* and inspired by that same *Spirit* came to the temple, Israel's house of *prayer*, and blessed God in these words: "Now you may dismiss your servant as you promised, God" (Luke 2:29).

The prophetess, Anna, is described as someone who "was constantly in the temple, worshipping day and night in fasting and *prayer*" (Luke 2:37).

And, even though Luke does not say so, early Christian piety and art always depicted Mary at *prayer* when the angel Gabriel appears to her and announces the birth of Jesus.

No wonder the Gospel of Luke is called the Gospel of prayer and the Holy Spirit!

But, we must ask the three obvious questions (two now and one later on): What is prayer as defined by Luke? And who is the Holy Spirit as defined by Luke?

To spare you the suspense, let me answer these first two questions and then proceed to explain my answer: For St. Luke, prayer is being available to God! And the Holy Spirit is the activity of God on earth! Luke's message with this theme is that when *you* are available to God, God acts in and through *you* to our world.

Luke shows us in two short chapters a world of people available to God. They, like us, have free will and could choose otherwise—but they didn't, with one exception—Zechariah, who, when he lacked trust, became mute, and when he regained that trust, became prolific. In every case, the choice Luke's characters make is rewarded not only by receiving the revelation, but by becoming the media through whom this revelation comes in the flesh.

Luke, who is always teaching his audience with his Gospel, is teaching us that when we are available to God in prayer, God's activity becomes possible in us—and in that case, everything becomes possible:

—a virgin becomes a wellspring of life...

—the barren become fertile...

—old extinguished people generate new life...

—an unwed mother finds a husband...

—old age recognizes youth...

—the outcast receives the message and sign...

—a poor baby is swaddled...

—the little people have a savior...

—the last are first...

—the lowest are highest...

—the least are known by name...

—force dwells in weakness...

—the world is upside down!

For Luke, God's revelation in Jesus has turned the world upside down! And the world turns upside down when these two converging forces intertwine: the openness of people—*prayer*; and the activity of God—*the Holy Spirit*. These two forces can overcome a world of strife, a posture of despair, an attitude of low self-esteem.

Zechariah, Elizabeth, Mary, the shepherds, Simeon, and Anna are also parts of myself. In fact, I am them myself: that barren one, burnt out, the doubter, the person who needs a sign, who is on the fringe, out in left field, not belonging somewhere, different, a guest in my own house; or old and tired, even if we are young or in the prime of life. Each of us knows only too well these parts in ourselves where we are barren and empty, can no longer go on, where we are lame and cannot succeed in this or that, where nothing comes out of us—parts in us where we are already finished living, vulnerable and impotent—parts of you where you know you are a stranger, out in the cold, pushed aside, misunderstood and apparently not understandable—there where you do not succeed in saying what you mean or being what you dream, because you are so much a shepherd. In each of us, there is a barren spot where we suffer hunger and thirst and cannot make it clear to anyone just how dark and painful and embarrassing and how cold it is there.

Well, it is for people such as these that the Gospel of Luke has been written—written for all people—for you and me. Luke has not only turned the world upside down, he has turned people inside out. He gives us a narrative to show us that it is precisely there inside each one of us where **we** can be found and recognized. Perhaps it is inside, where I have experienced grief and emptiness, that I can become comfort or life for another. No one really knows where we are fertile or how to give life or where we become father or mother. No one knows where his or her virginity lies.

For Luke, being open and available to God in *prayer* allows us to be transformed by God's *Holy Spirit*. It allows us to be turned upside down and inside out. For Luke, this is the mystery of humanity becoming receptacles for divine activity.

And now, it is time to turn to the third and final question in this sermon: What does it mean to be available to God? According to Luke, being available to God means being available to each other—with every hardship and joy that brings—with every wonder and pain we might experience.

The Gospel of Luke is the story of God becoming available to us. Let us make that story **live** by being available to God!

39.
JESUS AS PROPHET IN LUKE

Readings: Nehemiah 8:1-12 Psalm 19:8-12 Luke 4:14-21

What in this Gospel passage is so ordinary and common to a contemporary American audience that we would not even take notice of it—yet the Mediterranean culture of the first century would have taken significant note of this—and in fact, do so in the story we have from Luke? The same question could be asked of the passage from Nehemiah.

The answer is, of course, that Jesus could read! Ezra could read!

In today's world, about 25 percent of the world's adults are illiterate. In Jesus' day, around 90 percent of the people in Palestine were peasants. Only 10 percent were the elite. The number of people in either category who could read was rather limited.

That Jesus could read made him an exceptional person in his society. Notice how intent the people were—when he sat down everyone's eyes were fixed on him. They expected more. They expected that if he could read, he would also interpret the reading for them.

That Ezra could read made him an exceptional person in his society. Notice how long the people sat and listened to him read—from morning till midday. Today, we would not be able to sit still that long. We would be bored. Why could they stand such a long period of reading? Because for that society, reading was an art, almost entertainment, since it was such a rarity.

Jesus was rather aware that most of those around him were illiterate—notice his words: "Today this Scripture is fulfilled in your hearing." In Jesus' day Scripture was "heard" by the majority and "read" by the few who could also interpret it. Also notice in Nehemiah, that the crowd is described as men, women, and those children who could "understand"—not those who could "read," but those who could "understand."

The danger for our world is that most of us can read. We pick up the Scripture or the Bible at will and read it on our own. We don't need someone to read it for us or to us and also we are tempted to interpret it alone (simply because we can read).

The problem now becomes obvious: we who "read" a passage of Scripture that was written in a different culture, by a different people, in a different age are prone to "interpret" the passage through *our* contemporary cultural glasses.

The result is: we abort the original intention of the author and adjust the meaning of the passage to fit *our* culture's categories. It is not our intention to do this—we do not choose to change the meaning of Scripture—we are simply products of our own culture, our own time, our own categories, perceiving and understanding things *our* way.

Please notice that I am not saying one culture is right and one is wrong. I am only saying that all cultures are different.

Therefore, if I am aware that my Scripture (which I call the word of God, in which I place my faith, through which I come to salvation) was written in a different culture than my own, then to better understand that Scripture, I should study the cultural context in which it was written, so as to have a more complete idea of what it means.

For us who call ourselves Christian, Scripture is sacred. For us Christians who live two thousand years away from the culture that produced the Scripture, life is different. A Scripture that was written two thousand years ago can become sacred only when we attempt to combine our interpretation today with what the original author intended. A careful integration of two such diverse cultures requires a lot of time, effort, and energy to study and research the Bible in light of today's scholarship.

My exhortation to you, then, is to do this: if you hold this Bible to be sacred—if this Scripture is God's word for you—then it is worth all the effort, time, and energy you can give to increase its meaning in your life!

40.
THE ACTS OF THE APOSTLES

Reading: Acts 2:42-47; 4:32-37; 5:12-16

This book of the New Testament has always been thought to be a continuation of the Gospel of Luke since it was probably written by whoever wrote the Gospel. It was most likely written in Greece between the years 80-85 CE. The purpose of this book is to continue Luke's story about the origin and growth of Christianity under the guidance of the Spirit. It carries on the historical drama of the Gospel spelling out in detail, through the prime witnesses of Peter and Paul, how the word of God spread from Jerusalem to "the ends of the earth."

From this book, we get a picture of the life, growth, and problems of the earliest communities of Christians. We see *how* they lived, *what* they did and *why* they lived this way. We hear lines like:

"The community of believers was of one heart and one mind."

"With power, the apostles bore witness to the resurrection of the Lord Jesus."

"The Church was at peace, being built up and making steady progress in the fear of the Lord."

"At the same time, the Church enjoyed the consolation from the Holy Spirit."

It is no wonder, then, that in the history books of the times, people are quoted as saying about the early Christians: "Look at those Christians—see how they love one another."

The life led by the first communities of Christians was immediately inspired by Jesus himself. They lived as he lived—with love—selfless—concerned—persecuted—in the Spirit—in his Spirit. They lived as he taught them to live—giving of everything they had to the poor and needy—blessing and breaking bread with such a zeal and fervor that one would think Jesus had never died and gone away. But, because they lived this way—he lived. Because they lived as he did—he was resurrected in their midst—he lived in them. Because they gave of themselves, even to death in prisons and arenas—Jesus lived all over again. What he meant to them, he still meant to all people who came in contact with them. They were completing the work he had come to do—they were completing Christ himself. They had become his body—his risen body—living on—resurrected—in this world.

And so it is, even now, two thousand years later...Jesus is risen only if we make it so. He is risen—not because we preach it from a pulpit or we sing and pray it or we read it on a banner. He can be risen in our world only if we make him present by the way we live. If we live like him—then he will live.

But, you ask, "How can we live when life is so unsure, so vengeful, so up and down?" Sure, there are pressures and responsibility in being a Christian. Sure, there are frustrations in loving our neighbor. Sure, there are risks to entering relationships and raising a family. Sure, we get hurt when we give of ourselves or stand up for what we believe in. But, that's what we must do—that's how we must live—this is what he asks of those who wish to live like him. This is what he asks of us—we who bear his name and call ourselves "Christian"...

And, if *we* accept—then, **he is risen!**

41.

A COMPARISON OF THE GOSPELS OF MARK AND JOHN

I believe by comparing and contrasting these two Gospels, you will remember a lot about both of them—and this will be helpful since both Gospels span much of the New Testament era showing the development that happened during that time:

- Mark was written between 70-75 CE and John between 90-100 CE
- Mark is the shortest Gospel having 16 chapters and John is the longer of the two having 21 chapters
- Mark calls his work a "Gospel" and John doesn't classify his work at all
- Mark is writing to a Gentile audience in Rome and John writes to a mixed audience of Jew, Gentile, Samaritan, pagan, Greek, etc.
- Both authors are unknown to us
- Mark makes no eyewitness claims while John claims the eyewitness of the Beloved Disciple
- Mark uses the term "apostles" for the Twelve and John uses the term "disciples" for the Twelve
- Mark uses the word "Church" and John never uses it
- Mark names Jesus' mother as "Mary" and John never names her, but refers to her as "the mother of Jesus" and has Jesus always call her "woman"
- Mark writes his Gospel in story form to accompany the readings from the Torah in the synagogue and John writes theological treatises about Jesus explaining the "signs" of who Jesus is
- Mark's Gospel contains parables and miracle stories while in John there are no parables and he uses the term "signs" in place of "miracles"

- Mark's Gospel begins with Jesus' baptism and John's Gospel begins before the world began
- In Mark, Jesus is the Son of God proclaiming the Kingdom of God while in John, Jesus is the Word of God proclaiming himself
- Mark depicts a very human Jesus and John depicts Jesus as divine
- Mark uses a low Christology of Jesus as the expected Jewish Messiah and John uses a high Christology of Jesus as pre-existent, has divine powers and is "the way, the truth, and the life"
- Mark contains no hint of the history of the community that produced this Gospel while John combines the Jesus story along with the history of the community that produced his Gospel
- Mark is a one-author document written by a second-generation Christian and John is a multi-strata composition of at least three authors: the original document, the Evangelist, the disciples' additions

Conclusions:

The further away we get from any experience or event, the more we learn about it. We know more today about the first century of the Common Era in Israel than the people who lived at that time. People one thousand years from now will know more about us than we do about ourselves. This historical process includes experience, fact, witness, reflection, storytelling, dialogue, research, study, tradition—all of which leads us to faith—or not!

The distinct differences between the Gospels of Mark and John point up the historical process that went on between the years 75 and 95 CE. Over that short period of twenty years quite a few differences emerged in our early Church. Imagine the degree of differences between that first century CE and today, two thousand years later. Imagine the differences between your concepts of God as a child and what they are now! Imagine the differences between a woman's concept of God and a man's! Imagine the differences between a heterosexual's concept of God and a homosexual's! Imagine the differences between a Jew's concept of God and a Christian's! Imagine the differences between your concept of God and mine!

If you would ask John who Jesus was—he would give you a totally different answer than Mark—and he does—just as Mark's view of Jesus differs from Paul's and they all differ from our view of Jesus today. However, distinguish between the truth and ways of telling the truth. John and Mark tell us the *same* truth about Jesus. He is the One who has the words of eternal life—yet Mark and John tell us in two different ways.

A living faith changes. Don't be afraid of these changes or differences (Mark and John weren't). Welcome them (changes and differences): Mark **and** John—two **different** Gospels! Only then will you come to the truth!

42.

GOSPEL OF JOHN, CHAPTER SIX I

Readings: II Kings 4:42-44 Psalm 23 John 6:1-21

The theme of this chapter in John's Gospel is Jesus as the Bread of Life. Let me begin by explaining the structure of this chapter as we find it.

John sets up two stories followed by a discourse or speech by Jesus on bread. The first story is the multiplication of the loaves and the fishes. In this story, John exploits the symbolic potential of the same story found in the other Gospels. He does this on two levels at once—on one level all the images in Psalm 23 can be found in this story; on a second level he sets the scene on a mountain, which recalls Mt. Sinai and Moses in the Old Testament. In time or chronologically, he places this event near the feast of Passover. Jesus feeds the people symbolizing God who sends manna to the Israelites in the desert. But the actions of Jesus hint at something further as "he gives thanks," distributes the bread himself, and then gathers up the fragments that are left over. All in all, John begins this chapter with an emphasis on *bread*. This *sign*, for John, is clear: Jesus has power over bread!

The second story, like the first, is a familiar one in all the other Gospels. Did you notice, however, that John tells it rather briefly and matter-of-factly? He simply places Jesus walking on the water for no reason at all. Although, once again, he evokes that Old Testament theme of Moses leading the Israelites across the Red Sea. As in the first story, John here hints at something further since Jesus *walks on* the water to lead his apostles to the safe, dry, "promised" land. This story does not deal with water as in the Old Testament, but with Jesus himself, his very own *body*. This *sign*, for John again, is clear: Jesus has power over his body!

Two *signs*—two stories—filled with symbolism, and yet for John, incomplete. Their true significance is not yet revealed until the discourse of Jesus that follows. In this discourse, which will begin with the next homily, John climaxes the revelation of Jesus as the "Bread of Life." The power Jesus manifested over bread and over his body is now made obvious as Jesus calls himself "bread"—the bread of life—more than the manna offered by Moses in the desert, of which you could take no more than needed. Of this bread, you can take as much as you want, for there is always some left over. Unlike the manna in the desert, this bread remains forever.

In conclusion, I would like to return to the first story, the multiplication of the loaves and fishes. This is a story of abundance, of having more than you need. I would like to ask you a question about this story: Was it foolish of Jesus to try to feed that large crowd with those few loaves and fishes? Yet, he did it. He took the risk. He gave of what little he had and produced such an abundance that there was still some left over. In this very first story of chapter six, we can see that Jesus is bread—willing to share—willing to be shared, giving whatever he can to his fellow human beings. It is not until he gives what little he has that the *sign* of abundance really happens. You will notice that, unlike the other Evangelists, John never uses the word "miracle." He always calls what everyone else calls a "miracle" a *sign*. For John, these are *signs* of **who** Jesus is. They are significant in that they point to **who** Jesus is and not what Jesus did or performed. In this Gospel, as well as the other three, faith lies in **who** Jesus is and not what Jesus did.

In the passages ahead in chapter six, the words of Jesus will invite us to eat of the Bread of Life—to partake of his body. Accepting this invitation will result in eternal life. Then learn well from this story: when *we* are willing to take the risk of giving what little we have, *we* become like bread, broken and shared, passed around, eaten up, given away...

And as *we* are consumed, *we* will bring joy to others, *we* will satisfy their hunger, and *we* will nourish them so that they too are able to give to others. This is abundance! This is **who we are**! This is eternal life!

43.

GOSPEL OF JOHN, CHAPTER SIX II

Readings: Exodus 16:2-4, 12-15 John 6:24-50

We return to our trip through chapter six of John's Gospel dealing with the theme of Jesus as the Bread of Life. Recall these words from the Book of Exodus: "In the evening twilight you shall eat flesh, and in the morning you shall have your fill of bread, so that you may know that I, the Lord, am your God." This same promise is offered in John's Gospel: "Your ancestors ate the manna in the desert, but they died; this is the bread that comes down from heaven so that one may eat it and not die."

The greatest promises that have ever been extended to people are contained in these passages. At first, one might not readily grasp the sameness or similarity in these passages, and this is why I chose to repeat them and now to offer some observations about them.

It was in the darkness that the man Jesus was captured, crucified, and died. It was in the darkness that he said: "Take and eat, this is my body—take and drink, this is my blood." It was in the darkness that he lived—not knowing, wandering, questioning. All his life, he sought to become more and more someone who lived for others.

But all of his life was spent in darkness, groping and waiting, not being sure: "Father, if it is possible, let this cup pass from me." Unsure... willing...unwilling...convinced...reluctant! How could he really know the full meaning as he said: "I, myself, am the Bread of Life"? Morning had not yet come—he was still the flesh of the evening twilight, his old self, perishable food...for he still had to die. However, when the light of morning dawned, when, on the third day he rose...then he became the food that remains unto eternal life...then he became our bread...now we know and believe that he is the Lord our God!

And so, now, each day, we live with this hope, because we believe that we shall never be hungry, we shall never thirst. But...what about us?...Here we are in darkness...not really knowing, wandering around, questioning. We work and sweat and provide food for ourselves and others. We could say about the bread on the table in our homes, as we share it and break it, "Here, this is me—this is my body!" We become each other's bread and wine! We go through life in the dark—groping, waiting, not being sure, and we sometimes wish, "Let this cup pass from me!" Unsure...unwilling...convinced...reluctant...and then what?...Will our hopes be really fulfilled?...Will the morning dawn for you and me?

44.
GOSPEL OF JOHN, CHAPTER SIX III

Readings: Proverbs 9:16 John 6:51-58

Why is it that every time Christians gather in church, they do the same two things over and over? They speak words, and then they break bread. The words change every week, but the *sign* of breaking bread never changes. It is always done, has always been done, and as far as we can tell, it will continue to be done. Why different words, but always the same *sign*?

The discourse set up by John the Evangelist may offer some meaning to our weekly gathering and to our lives.

In this discourse, John climaxes his revelation of Jesus as the "Bread of Life." Jesus calls himself "bread"—the Bread of Life—more than the manna offered by Moses in the desert, of which you could take no more than needed. Of *this* bread, you can take as much as you want. Not like the manna our ancestors ate, but *this* bread remains forever.

Jesus calls himself "bread," the most elementary food for people on earth. Some of you may have heard about or even experienced the "bread lines" in our streets toward the end of the last World War. Bread, then, was about the only thing people lived for. As long as there was bread, there was a chance for survival. In those days, bread was life, the separation between life and death. Even today, in our land of wealth and abundance, there are "bread lines." In Washington, D.C., and in some of our southern states, this phenomenon of the past is still experienced by many people who do not have enough food to live on. Go out into your own city, in the poorer areas, to see this phenomenon locally. And who knows, the future may hold the same experience for us all.

Also in the Bible, bread is life...the source of life...the "Bread of Eternal Life." The vision John presents is that of a man who is bread, which I can take and break and eat...in which I can taste life.

Bread is many things: Breakable—wanting to be eaten—one from many grains—warm—fragile—seed in the ground—life and death. Many things were said of Jesus: that he walked on the water—made the blind see—that he forgave sins—that he is a shepherd, a light, a lamb. But, he calls himself bread.

John does not have a fuller sign than this. It is on our tables every day—we share it—we break it for ourselves and those we love. The bread we earn, we give to others, as if it were ourselves, something of our own life. Jesus blessed and broke bread over and over again. Maybe this is why we Christians do it over and over each week...for this is life: To be, and do, as he did—to be bread for others—to be broken—eaten—shared—given away—to die in order to live.

Some cookbooks will tell you to knock on bread when it is baking to hear whether it is done. You could also knock on him, and if you listen well, you will hear life...perhaps eternal life...perhaps God!

45.
THE BODY OF CHRIST IN JOHN'S GOSPEL

Reading: John 2:13-25

In the Gospel of John every appearance of Jesus in Jerusalem was symbolic, demonstrative, and significant! The stories of Jesus' time in Jerusalem in John's Gospel will be a time and place that manifests God's saving actions in and through Jesus, the mercy and faithfulness of God in our midst.

This story in chapter two takes place in Jerusalem, within the temple precincts, the center of the Jewish world, in the midst of the hostile environment of the citadel of ecclesiastical authority. Here we see a unique characterization of Jesus as an angry prophet who symbolically destroys the temple with a whip. He drives out not only people (merchants, money changers, and clergymen), but also animals. Recall now that it was near the Passover—and what is Passover without lambs and other animals to be sacrificed for the feast? No orthodox Jew would eat a lamb at Passover unless it was slaughtered in the temple, which was the place of sacrifice for the paschal lamb.

For John, the author of this story, the removal of the animals from the temple by Jesus signifies Jesus as the new paschal lamb. The Evangelist is using this story to illustrate the replacing of the old covenant with a new one, the old sacrifice with a new one—replacing the blood of an animal with the life of a person: Jesus himself! This fourth Gospel is unfortunately supersessionistic—the author of this Gospel wanted nothing to do with Judaism. Therefore, in John we find an ongoing "replacement theology." In this Gospel, Jesus replaces everyone and everything in the Old Testament.

However, for Jesus, the temple was primarily the house of his Father. God was present in the temple! God was present in the ark of the covenant in which the Torah, the sacred law of Israel was kept. This holy ark was in the temple and that guaranteed God's presence in the temple. In this sense, Jesus calls the temple his Father's house. Wherever the covenant is most evident, there is God.

More directly than the hidden meaning I just mentioned is the fact that in the story Jesus refers to *himself* as the "temple." John wishes to show Jesus as the new temple, replacing, destroying, and fulfilling the old one. His reference: "Destroy this temple" is referring to this house of God, his body. John is making it clear that the old temple was destroyed to make way for a new one—Jesus' very own body. For the Christian, Jesus is the new and perfect dwelling place of God! It is in him, in his body, in his life of unending service where we find God. He is also the temple, also the Paschal Lamb, also the covenant. Not only through the blood of animals, but through him, we worship the Father. Not only with the law of Moses, but with him, we live out the covenant. Not only in a temple or tabernacle, but in him, we find God.

We who call ourselves Christian, the Church—we are his body living on in this world. As Paul says to the church in Corinth: "You are the body of Christ" (I Cor. 12:27), and to the same church he says, "Do you not know that your body is the temple of the Holy Spirit" (I Cor. 6:19)?

Therefore,

If we want to find God, we must find people first.

If we want to live out our covenant with God, we must learn to love one another.

If we want to be like God, we must become **human!**

46.

THE LETTER OF PAUL TO PHILEMON

Reading: The entire Letter of Paul to Philemon

Now, let's do a little **exegesis**: Who is Philemon? Who is Onesimus? What relationship is there among Paul, Philemon, and Onesimus? What is the story behind this letter? To answer these questions, we must examine two theories of exegesis.

The older theory says that Philemon was a wealthy Greek slave owner who was a Christian and coworker of Paul. Onesimus was a runaway slave from Philemon's household. Paul comes upon Onesimus in prison, converts him to Christianity, baptizes him, and now sends him back to Philemon with a letter after his release from prison.

The newer theory says that Philemon and Onesimus are blood brothers. Somewhere in their past, Onesimus committed an injustice against Philemon for which he had failed to compensate him. As in the older theory, Paul and Onesimus meet in prison where Paul is able to convert him to Christianity and baptizes him. Paul, thrown into prison, could no longer work with Philemon on the common task of Christianity. So Paul sends the surrogate whom he had just baptized, Onesimus, Philemon's brother. Paul writes a letter to Philemon in which he hopes to reconcile the two brothers.

The newer theory, found in a book entitled *Embassy of Onesimus* by Allen Dwight Callahan, shows that verse 16 of the Letter to Philemon has been inadequately and inaccurately translated and thus the older interpretation ensued for the past two thousand years. Dr. Callahan, who is assistant professor of New Testament at Harvard Divinity School, calls our attention to verse 16 of the letter where two terms are often inaccurately translated. On page 44 of his book, he points out that *as a slave* in Greek really has the force of "as though a slave" (*hos doulos*). And on page 49 he says, "So Paul insists that Onesimus be received no longer as a slave (*ouketi os doulon*), i.e., an alien to Philemon's household of faith, but as a beloved brother (*alla...adelphon agapeton*)."

The second phrase that is often inaccurately translated is *as a man,* which is literally in Greek "in the flesh." "In the flesh" means biologically. If Philemon knows Onesimus "in the flesh," it means they are blood brothers. Now that Onesimus has been baptized, Paul insists, they are brothers literally and spiritually.

And now, let us do a little **hermeneutics**: How do we apply this letter to our own lives today?

If we accept the older theory, we could discern a message of equality among all Christians no matter their status. Paul backs this up in another of his letters where he says: "In Christ there is no slave nor free" (Gal. 3:28). But this older theory carries a fundamental flaw in it: Paul, having the chance, never condemns slavery. This is most unusual for a Jew and a Christian!

If we accept the newer theory (supported by Dr. Callahan's book) the message for us is given in his book as, "Justice at its best is love correcting everything that stands against love" (A quote taken from Martin Luther King, Jr., by Callahan). In other words, the Gospel or good news of reconciliation is being proclaimed in this letter of Paul.

As we continue to apply this good news to our own lives, it is as though Paul condemns Christians who find it easy to forgive everyone and anyone except the members of their own families, their siblings, and their parents.

Family problems are often the hardest to solve since family relationships are so close and so intense (we have them from birth to death—they permeate everything we are and do—they permeate every moment of our existence). Paul reminds Philemon (and us), "Charity begins at home." We did not choose our parents or siblings. They did not choose us. We are given to each other by God. It's often easier to forgive and love the friends *we* have chosen. The more difficult task is to love and honor those who have been given to us, to remain faithful to them all our life. Friends come and go. Family is eternal. What we do with our family is the true test of our Christian commitment to justice, love, forgiveness, and new life.

Those among us who have left family and home for the first time will find today's Scripture poignant! Those of us who are living far from our relatives and friends, as well as those of us who have lost parents or siblings in death will also find a great deal of truth in this letter.

The Letter to Philemon, a *little* letter with a *big* message!

47

THE LETTER OF JAMES I

Reading: James 1:1-27

Let me begin by asking, "James who?" There are two apostles of Jesus with the name James (James, the brother of John, and James Alphaeus). There is also James, "the brother of the Lord" (Bishop of Jerusalem) known as "James the Righteous."

Scholars date this letter around 90 CE, and that makes the author unknown and perhaps a disciple of James.

The audience to whom this letter is addressed is "the twelve tribes in the diaspora." This letter is called a "catholic epistle" because it is written to the *whole* Church and not just one specific Christian community, as in almost all the other New Testament writings.

Because of its late date, the author cannot be any of the Jameses who lived at Jesus' time, but perhaps someone who used James the Brother of the Lord as an inspiration and might have even known James when he was alive. Material in the letter shows a date later than the time of James (40-50 CE) and the diaspora (70 CE). Perhaps it was written during the persecution under the Emperor Domitian (81-96 CE).

The contents of this letter include twelve topics. Let us look at one of these up close: "Humbly welcome the word that has been planted in you, and is able to save your souls. Be doers of the word and not hearers only, deluding yourselves."

Cardinal John Henry Newman of nineteenth-century England once commented on this letter and especially these particular verses in one of his sermons. Newman sets out three groups of Christians:

1. Those who are open sinners who care neither to profess nor practice their faith.

2. At the other extreme, those who both profess and perform the Gospel truths.

3. And in-between those two extremes are the majority of Christians who profess, but inconsistently perform or in one vital area or another just weakly perform their faith—in other words, lukewarm Christians (like those being referred to in the Letter of James).

Listen to how Cardinal Newman describes this third group:

"I say plainly...though it is a serious thing to say, that the aim of most men esteemed conscientious and religious...is, to all appearance, not how to please God, but how to please themselves without displeasing Him...that they make the world the first object in their minds, and use religion as a corrective, a restraint, upon too much attachment to the world. They think that religion is a negative thing, a sort of moderate love of the world, a moderate luxury, a moderate avarice, a moderate ambition, and a moderate selfishness" (Pastoral Sermons iv. 26, 28, 29).

Newman spent most of his writings and preaching addressing this third and largest group of lukewarm Christians. Now the big question for us today is, into which of these three groups do we personally fall?

James, Newman and almost every Evangelist in Christian history have spent most of their energy trying to convert those lukewarm Christians.

Again—Into which of these groups do *you* personally fall?

48.
THE LETTER OF JAMES II

Readings: James 2:14-26 Mark 8:27-35

The Letter of James asks, "What good is it, my brothers and sisters, if someone says he has faith but does not have works?" He then concludes, "Faith without works is dead." But notice what he means by practice of faith—he does not refer to attending religious services, but rather meeting the needs of people in distress. In the Gospel of Mark, Jesus does the same—after eliciting a verbal profession of faith on the part of Peter and the apostles, he concretizes that faith by asking them that if they really believe; and if they really want to follow him, they must deny themselves and take up their cross.

But what good is a cross? It is like a statue you hang on your wall or in a Church. What good is a cross if you only *have* it? It causes only frustration and misery, confusion and doubt, depression and rebellion. There is no glory in having a cross! The glory can come only when we "take up" that cross and follow Jesus.

There are many crosses in life: To lose your job or suffer the death of a loved one—to live a life rejected by one's family and friends—to be physically or mentally handicapped, to be poor, to be lonely—to be denied the fullness of life because of sex or the color of your skin—to be widowed or divorced—to grow old without the company of family and friends—to be ridiculed or repressed because of your convictions and beliefs—to be homeless—to suffer some physical ailment or mental anxiety.

Faith is holding on desperately to life whether it favors us or not. Faith is living in spite of life's crosses, in spite of death. Faith is "taking up" your cross. Faith is being lifted up on the cross so as to see better why you must live. Faith is opening wide your arms to embrace your brothers and sisters in need. Faith is nailing yourself to your cross as your only way of salvation. Faith is shivering at the thought that we have no glory but the cross of Jesus, the Lord.

Our Faith has a name—we call it Christianity—named after *his* way of life, the way, the truth, and the life. Being a Christian means being called to imitate Jesus' fidelity to the human condition. Being Christian means to take up *our* cross and challenge death wherever it presents itself, above all when it is the result of inability or refusal to love. Loving with the love of Jesus means forgiving those who crucify you. It means loving another in full recognition of his or her otherness, even across all the barriers that people never cease to build between themselves. It means loving down to the very roots of hostility and sin that make an enemy of the other—creating unity at the precise point of alienation. It means never to be indifferent to life! It means embracing the suffering that rejection by others will bring—the sentence to death for having loved—the actual dying.

At one point in his life, Scripture tells us that Jesus said, "Love one another as I have loved you," that is, to the point of laying down our lives. And if our faith allows us to live this way we will experience what it means to live, to be human. It is not some religious act that proves the faith of a Christian, but rather participation in the sufferings of God in the life of the world. This kind of living gives hope to others—this kind of love is victorious—for this kind of suffering and death are productive of life—as we have heard him say, "Whoever loses his life for my sake and that of the gospel will save it." To die is to live—the paradox of life that we Christians not only believe in, but must live out.

Perhaps, these words do not affect you. Perhaps you can see no risk to the Christian faith. Then I can make only one suggestion: try to live it and see for yourself!

49.
THE BOOK OF REVELATION

Reading: Revelation 7:1-17

P robably one of the most obscure books of the entire Bible is the Book of Revelation. Yet, today, with the rise of Christian fundamentalism, this book has received more attention than any other in both the Hebrew and Christian Scriptures.

As with every book of the Bible, there is much we do not know about Revelation. At the same time, there is a lot we do know. Scholars in both the Protestant and Catholic traditions have probed this book for centuries, but only in recent times, with the coming of "form critique" have they been able to make any sense out of this book.

There is no way, in this one homily, that we could investigate all your questions about the Book of Revelation, so we will stick to the passage above and see what meaning it offers to us.

The person who wrote this book—John is his name, but not to be confused with the apostle nor the writer of the Gospel of John—is a visionary who writes down in understandable symbols the content of the visions he is receiving. His vision or "revelation" is a simple one— that the Kingdom of God is inaugurated by Jesus, perpetuated by the Church and protected by God from worldly enemies. The other element of this vision is that the fulfillment of the kingdom will come very soon with Jesus' return—thus the other name often used for this book, The Apocalypse. *Apocalypse* means that which must take place soon.

The author and visionary, John, has chosen very obvious and common symbols to convey to his Christian audience the mystery of the Kingdom of God. He took the most common elements of Christian life at that time and used these to describe the meaning of his visions. Those elements and symbols were the ceremonies of and the functions played by Christians during the Mass, the liturgy around the year 90 CE when this book was written. Therefore, what sounds like a description of heaven and the kingdom is really a description of what that Christian community was doing at Mass in the years 90 to 96 CE. Let's take a closer look.

Let's begin with those *angels* that seem to be all over the place. One angel brings the seal of God while crying out to four other angels not to do any harm to those who are about to receive the seal. The angels are symbolic of those members of that Christian community who were assigned to carry out specific duties during the Mass (somewhat like altar servers or acolytes do today). One brings the seal while four others guard the doors of the place where they are celebrating Mass to keep out enemies or anti-Christian spies. The *seal* of the living God is oil to be placed on the foreheads of those about to be baptized. The *144,000* from every tribe of Israel are those members who are being baptized into this particular Christian community during the Mass. The number is reached by going 12 x 12 x 1000. The first 12 is symbolic of the 12 Tribes of Israel. The second 12 is symbolic of the perfection they enter with baptism. The 1000 is a number used simply to mean a large number. So we simply conclude that a large number of Jews were being baptized into Christianity and thus enter the Kingdom of God.

Next, there is a *huge crowd, which no one could count*—obviously the reference made to Abraham in Genesis when God promises that he would father all nations (not just Jews) into the kingdom. This group is standing before the *throne* and the *lamb*. In the liturgy of the Mass, who sits on a throne? The bishop, of course. The lamb is a symbol of the altar on which the Eucharist is celebrated. This crowd is already dressed in *long white robes* and holding *palm branches*. In other words, this crowd is the already baptized members of the community (the congregation)—white robes were given in the ceremony of baptism in the early Church. The fact that they are carrying palm branches suggests two things: that they are victorious and triumphed over evil in the waters of baptism, and also a symbol of the fate that awaited many professed Christians in those days—that of martyrdom.

Next, these groups begin to sing back and forth to one another—not unlike our own liturgies where we alternate verses of hymns or dialogue with the leader in prayer. Reference is then made, to *all the angels* standing around the throne—obviously the acolytes serving or incensing the bishop—along with *elders*, a title given to priests in the New Testament, and *the four living creatures,* symbolic of the presence of God, with four attributes of knowledge, strength, awesomeness, and omnipresence.

Finally, one of the elders or priests asks John, the author, who the congregation is. The elder then proceeds to describe them as "the ones who have survived the great period of trial and have washed their robes and made them white in the blood of the lamb" (Rev. 7:14). In other words: Pagans, Jews, Greeks, Gentiles, etc. who were tested and found worthy to be baptized into Christianity and receive the Eucharist—the symbol of full participation not only in the Church, but also in the Kingdom of God.

Therefore, the vision that John saw of the Kingdom of God has been transmitted to us in liturgical symbols with apocalyptic language. We have here an obvious description of the celebration of a Mass around the year 90 CE in which a large number of Jews were about to be baptized into Christianity and join the ranks of that local Christian congregation.

Cryptic language is always a product in time of persecution. This language is strong in the Book of Revelation and has no other intent than to decoy the oppressors, who in those days were the Romans. This is another good example of apocalyptic writing in the Bible. There is no intent in this book to predict the future or project itself into a world beyond its time. Be careful of any interpretations that do this!

50.
THE MOST ESSENTIAL QUESTION OF THE NEW TESTAMENT:
AN ANALYSIS

The most essential question of the New Testament is: **Who is Jesus?** Not, where did he live? How old was he? Who were his grandparents? Etc. The five major authors as well as all the other writers in the New Testament have given us a wealth of material to ponder the answer to this question along with the question itself. Let me conclude this volume by giving you an analysis of how this was done by the five major authors: Paul, Mark, Matthew, Luke, and John.

As you know, the seven letters found in the New Testament which are authentic to the Apostle Paul are: Romans, I Corinthians, II Corinthians, Galatians, Philippians, I Thessalonians, and Philemon. As Paul attempts to deal with this question, as well as to try to answer it, he never gives his readers any biographical information about Jesus other than his death and resurrection. This is Paul's outstanding answer to the question: "Paul, a slave of Christ Jesus, called to be an apostle and set apart for the gospel of God, which he promised previously through his prophets in the holy scriptures, the gospel about his Son, descended from David according to the flesh, but established as **Son of God** in power according to the spirit of holiness through resurrection from the dead, Jesus Christ our Lord" (Rom. 1:1-4). And so, Paul tells his readers that Jesus is son of David, according to the flesh, and has become Son of God by virtue of his resurrection. All through Paul's writings, which are the oldest in the New Testament, dating from around 50-64 CE, he gives very little about Jesus' life except that he who was crucified is now risen from the dead.

The next author in sequence would be the writer of the Gospel of Mark, which we date somewhere between 70-75 CE. Mark begins his Gospel, "The beginning of the gospel of Jesus Christ, the **Son of God**"

(Mark 1:1). He tells us of Jesus' death and resurrection, but then adds much more to his Gospel, including stories about Jesus' ministry, with miracles, parables, and teachings, and begins his story with the baptism of Jesus: "Jesus came from Nazareth of Galilee and was baptized in the Jordan by John. On coming up out of the water he saw the heavens being torn open and the Spirit, like a dove, descending upon him. And a voice came from the heavens, 'You are my beloved Son; with you I am well pleased'" (Mark 1:9-11). Mark tells us much more than Paul about Jesus' life and takes us back as far as his baptism.

The second Gospel is written by Matthew and is dated somewhere between 80-85 CE. He too tells of Jesus' death and resurrection, like Paul and Mark, and also about his ministry and baptism, as did Mark. But then Matthew adds a whole infancy narrative and takes us back to the birth of Jesus including a long genealogy. Here is how he begins his Gospel: "The book of the genealogy of Jesus Christ, the son of David, the son of Abraham" (Matt. 1:1). Using his knowledge of the Hebrew Scriptures (II Sam. 7:8-17), Matthew equates "son of David" with **Son of God**. Matthew is telling his readers and us that Jesus is Son of God at his birth.

The third Gospel writer, Luke, comes on the scene at almost the same time as Matthew, somewhere around 85 CE. His Gospel contains all the biographical data of the previous three authors, but then he takes us back to Jesus' conception. The angel Gabriel tells Mary: "The Holy Spirit will come upon you, and the power of the Most High will overshadow you. Therefore, the child to be born (to you) will be called holy, the **Son of God**" (Luke 1:35).

Finally, somewhere between the years 90-100 CE, a fourth Gospel is written by the author(s) we now call John. This Gospel contains the death and resurrection of Jesus, his ministry, refers to his baptism and birth, but then plummets us back before the world began. This Gospel tells us that Jesus was Son of God in the beginning, at the creation of the world. In the beautiful hymn that opens this Gospel, John tells us: "In the beginning was the Word, and the Word was with God...And the Word became flesh and made his dwelling among us, and we saw his glory, the glory as of the Father's only Son" (John 1:1,14). Using wisdom images from the Hebrew Scriptures, John is equating "Word" with **Son of God**.

Now, there you have it. Have you noticed what's been happening from writer to writer, as well as the time line of dates? The answer to the most essential question in the New Testament is the same for every author in the New Testament. Therefore, the question must be the same for each of them. But notice the differences when and where each of them places their answer.

So, what conclusions can we draw from all this? I think we can conclude that the further away we get from a historical event (such as the Jesus event), the more we learn about it. The longer we reflect on an event or experience, the more we have to say about it. The longer the early Christians told stories about Jesus, remembered Jesus, talked about Jesus, the more they came to grips with what was the essential question about him and what the answer to that question could be. They all answered that **Jesus is the Son of God.**

Paul and his Gentile Christians believed he became the Son of God at his resurrection. Mark and his community believed he became Son of God at his baptism. Matthew and his Jewish audience believed he became the Son of God at his birth. Luke and his Gentile converts believed he was Son of God from his conception. John and his disciples believed he was the Son of God before the world began.

The final conclusion we can come to is where all five authors agree. Not only do they all say that Jesus is the Son of God, but also that he died and rose from the dead. Notice that this belief is in every writing of the New Testament without distinction. We call this the *kerygma* of the faith. It is the core teaching of faith in Jesus. The word *kerygma* is the Greek root for our English word *kernel,* which means core or essence. This is the kernel of the Christian faith.

To conclude, then, let me return to the opening sermon of this book. **The Bible is a book of faith** in the one God, and the New Testament is the faith that **Jesus is the Son of God** and that **he died and rose from the dead!**